ADOPTION:

The Unpaved Road to Happiness

by Valerie Grissom

This book is based upon actual events, persons, and locations. However, some names and identifying details have been changed to protect the privacy of individuals. The author has chosen to use the name given to her by her birth mother before she was placed for adoption.

Published by Ionic Press
Oklahoma City, OK

IONIC

PRESS

Cover photos by Erin McCaffrey
www.mccaffreyphotography.com

Manufactured in the United States of America

DEDICATED TO:
Christopher and Abby

Chosen by God
to be chosen by us.

Romans 5: 1-5

Therefore, having been justified by faith, we have peace with God through our Lord Jesus Christ, through whom also we have access by faith into this grace in which we stand and rejoice in hope of the glory of God. Moreover, not only that, but we also glory in tribulations, knowing that tribulation produces perseverance; and perseverance, character; and character, hope.

2004

OUR JOURNEY BEGINS

1

ROGER & VALERIE

Roger and I both were the baby of our families. We both grew up living in somewhat of a bubble, everything we did within a few miles of home. My bubble was Oklahoma City, Roger's in Ardmore, Oklahoma. We each moved only once growing up, went to work before we were teenagers, and both suffered a loss at the age of twelve. Roger's father died, and I lost my sense of family security through divorce.

We grew up, attended rival Oklahoma universities, began our careers and settled into the lives we thought we were destined to live. Until, fate decided our paths should cross. I was thirty-three and Roger thirty-nine when we met on a blind date set up by mutual friends. We were both a bit skeptical about blind dates, so we agreed to meet just for coffee. However, what we had set up as an easy out if things weren't a match, turned into a seven-hour coffee date.

From the first date we both sensed the potential for a future together, and we wanted to know everything about each other's history. Though our personalities were different, we quickly discovered we had similar childhood experiences and circumstances in common.

In the past, I had gravitated to roller coaster relationships— full of highs and lows. However, when I met Roger, things were immediately different. It was like being on an elevated monorail – steady, smooth and constant. With him, I felt peace and stability.

Now both looking toward the future with happiness and excitement, we eloped after a year of dating, surprising friends and family, and awakening my spontaneous side.

* * *

From the first date, Roger knew how important my faith life was to me and that it was one thing I would never compromise. Through many discussions, Bible studies, prayers, meeting with priests, attending different churches and more prayers, we discovered the hidden treasure of the Greek Orthodox Church. Our decision to become members felt comfortable and spiritually fulfilling for both of us.

After our elopement, we were ready to grow as one in our hearts and minds. We joined the church together, and had our marriage blessed a lá *My Big Fat Greek Wedding*. Then, we both felt confident our marriage foundation was deeply rooted in Christ.

2
DINKS

Our early marriage exemplified the cliché--double income no kid couple (DINKS). We traveled on a whim, slept in, dined out, and discovered a new hobby together—water gardening. For five years, we doted on our dogs, and worked and played, enjoying our life together. Yet, the idea of having children was not totally out of our thoughts.

When two of our dogs passed away, the topic of children came up again. We had known from our first date that conceiving might not be possible for either of us. And, after a year or two of trying and not getting pregnant, testing confirmed that we were not able to have children.

We did not want to push the emotional, physical or financial drain of fertility treatments, but we would consider adoption. Or, maybe we weren't supposed to be parents and God had something else in store for us.

Unlike many of our friends who chose to pursue adoption, we decided in the beginning we were not willing to travel the globe in search of a child, or to apply to countless agencies hoping one would work out. We were also not willing to be an open checkbook by using an attorney to pair us with a birth mother. Finally, we applied to just one adoption agency. We chose Catholic Charities, where I had been adopted.

We met Sabra, the Adoption Coordinator and Social Worker at Catholic Charities. Private by nature, we were somewhat hesitant at first to open our lives up to the scrutiny required to be considered as prospective adoptive parents, including background checks, fingerprinting, home studies and invasive questioning.

Sabra immediately put us at ease and guided us through the process in a respectful manner. She had a soothing and calming temperament, exactly what we needed during our emotional whirlwind as prospective, adoptive parents.

After being approved by Catholic Charities to be classified officially as Prospective Adoptive Parents, we breathed a sigh of relief to have scaled that hurdle. Then, reality set in. Realizing our life was pretty darn good and how complicated children would make it, we decided to put off our adoption search a few more months for another round of fun and travel.

I called Sabra at Catholic Charities and had her place us in the inactive file, telling her we would let them know when we were ready to resume. We were in control of this process, and kids could wait. Or, so we thought.

3

THE CALL

Receiving the phone call from Sabra was quite a shock. My first reaction... *Catholic Charities actually went through the dead files? Why? Was it a sign? God's will? Roger and I had prayed for God's will. But up to this point, we weren't clear on which way we would be directed. We just prayed for it to be easy if it was His will, and difficult if it was not meant to be.*

I called Roger to tell him the news. It was a good thing he was sitting down, as Sabra had asked me if I was sitting down only moments before. We had been chosen by a birth mother, pregnant with twins, and due to deliver in a few months.

So this is how 'easy' looks when God drops babies in your lap? We didn't even need to put together an adoptive parent scrapbook. (Many couples agonize over these, making sure everything is perfect so they might be chosen by a teenage mother making her selection.)

The birth mother had also been adopted through Catholic Charities eighteen years before. When the birth mother had searched the files and not found any prospective parents with whom she felt a connection, Sabra had pulled out a few of the inactive files. The birth mother was immediately drawn to us; thrilled to discover that I had also been adopted through Catholic Charities. As Catholic Charities adoptees, we shared a special bond.

The birth mother also chose us over other couples because the birth father had a few drops of Indian blood, and was from the same tribe as Roger. *We had no idea how critical this would be when we began the adoption process.* So, she chose us-- sight and scrapbook unseen!

The birth mother knew adoption was what she wanted to do from the beginning, having been adopted herself. Abortion was never an option, and for that, we were grateful. On the other hand, Catholic Charities let us know the birth father was not yet on board with the adoption.

However, Catholic Charities thought there was little risk in moving forward considering the birth father's lack of any financial support during the birth mother's pregnancy. They felt that having the birth father's parental rights terminated would not be an issue for them, just a formality, and the twins would be eligible for adoption. This is what the birth mother wanted, and we were scheduled to meet her soon.

Journal - 01/15/04

My, how time flies! Within the last three weeks, we have received a call about a birth mother named Nicole who is pregnant with twins and due to deliver in two months. We are shocked, excited, and downright overwhelmed.

We had prayed that if it was God's will for us to adopt children, they would have to fall into our lap! So far, the process has been easier than going to the dentist. I prayed on Sunday for God to give us a sign if we were meant to adopt. The next day, Sabra called about the twins! We will pray that the birth father will accept Nicole's decision to place the children for adoption.

4

NICOLE

Nicole was sweet and respectful, though somewhat quiet and shy when we met her. We learned she had finished high school with straight A's. She had dated the birth father off and on, and knew him to be kind and generous. She had also been attracted to his rebellious side. She knew he drank and occasionally smoked pot; knew he had tattoos covering his body. However, she didn't know the full extent of his rebellion and drug use until their relationship had progressed too far, and she was pregnant.

At one point, they discussed marriage and being parents together. It sounded romantic, but they knew it was impossible. Nicole would only consider raising children with him if he moved out of his parent's house, got a job and got off drugs. With her due date quickly approaching, she had decided to call Catholic Charities.

Journal - 02/11/04

We met Nicole and her parents today. What kindness they exude. We can tell what loving parents they are to Nicole, and she is lucky to have them here to support her through this difficult time.

How hard it must have been for her to tell them she was pregnant. She was a good Catholic girl who had a lapse in judgment. Don't we all at one point in our lives? But she is paying dearly for it now.

Nicole is petite, with golden blonde hair, hazel eyes, and beautiful porcelain skin. We felt an instant connection between us. She is so smart. She likes math, Italian food, and playing the piano. We share a love of traveling to Italy. She is deliberate and thoughtful, mature and strong. We are blessed to have been chosen by her. I think it is a good match, a God wink. I can't believe she is due in a little over a month!

Journal - 03/08/04

We are nervous and excited. The due date has changed by a few days. We have loved the reaction from telling friends and family our exciting news about adopting the twins. We are already receiving hand-me-downs and baby beds, and showers are planned for us. Everyone's generosity is over the top, and a little overwhelming.

I love making lists! It keeps me sane. In my journal, I wrote:

- *Make childcare arrangements for when I have to go back to work*
- *Order birth announcements*
- *Add babies to health insurance*
- *Get another car seat*
  ...and to do when we get the babies!
- *Diapers, bottles, formula*
- *Bassinet*

The thought never occurred to me to put *Hire the best adoption attorney you can find* on the list.

5

THE DAY OUR LIVES
CHANGED FOREVER

Journal - 03/11/04

Nicole was going to be induced at 5:30 a.m. She was up at 3:30 a.m. to get to the hospital. She had a very easy labor and didn't need any pain medications until early in the afternoon. We got calls throughout the day on her progress, and by 3:15 p.m., she was ready! Roger and I rushed over to the hospital. By 3:45, she had baby boy Christopher, and thirty minutes later, she had baby girl Abby.

While the babies were being tested, cleaned up and weighed, we were able to see Nicole. She was doing fine. She was able to spend several hours with the babies before we went back to meet them.

When we saw them for the first time, we were so overwhelmed with joy and awe.

They had the cutest little pink and blue crocheted hats on their tiny heads. Only three hours old, baby Abby was wide-eyed and alert, following our voices and movements. She knew us by voice, as Nicole had recorded our voices and played the sounds to her pregnant belly.

Christopher was sacked out, having paved the way out of the womb for his little sister. (After getting to know Abby's little personality, we know she probably kicked Christopher out of the womb so she could have the place to herself for a while.)

Abby had a lot of dark hair and Christopher had very little hair, but his was light. We changed their little tiny shirts for the first time, touching that soft, new baby skin, and reluctantly pried ourselves away to let Nicole rest. They spent the night for the first and last time in the room with her.

Unfortunately, even though we already had Nicole's consent for adoption, we didn't immediately get to bring Christopher and Abby home with us. In order for the twins to be eligible for adoption, the birth father either had to voluntarily relinquish his parental rights, or have them terminated in court. Thankfully, Catholic Charities had a wonderful set of foster parents that came the day after the twins' birth, and took them temporarily into their home.

All along, Nicole had told us that she felt she had listened to God's will, and that we were the ones called to raise Christopher and Abby. Things were not good between her and the birth father, as he had not gotten a job, off drugs or out from under the roof of his parent's house. She knew her life was not meant to be spent with him, or for Christopher and Abby to be subjected to a life set up for difficulty, if not failure.

We are grateful that Nicole always had looked towards the future. To have understood the type of life Christopher and Abby would have faced living with a single mom too young to care for them, and a father incapable of providing them a safe and stable environment was very mature.

Up to this point, phone calls about our impending status of new parents were kept to a select few. But as the excitement and reality grew, so did time on the phone repeating the updates. It was time to take to the computer. Impersonal as it felt, spreading such personal information on a group email basis, it was worth it for efficiency.

Email Update - 03/24/04

Dear Friends and Family,

We got to see the twins today for a few hours. But we were too busy feeding them, changing diapers and just staring at them to take too many pictures. They are doing great. They are already growing out of their clothes!

It looks like there is no court date set to terminate the parental rights of the birth father. But hopefully the date will be set in the next week or so. The birth father still has not contacted the birth mother's attorney, so we hope that is good news.

The foster family that Christopher and Abby are staying with will be featured in an upcoming issue of the Sooner Catholic newspaper. These babies are numbers 150 and 151 that the foster family has cared for with NO compensation. They said the twins were some of the most peaceful children they have fostered. The babies are sleeping for four to five hours at night. They have to wake them up to feed them!

Already they have been to Mass, a wedding and a soccer game – and they are barely a week and a half old!

Birth mother is very peaceful too, and is already starting her studies again. Please keep them all in your prayers. We will keep you updated as we find out more!

Love,

Valerie, Roger, Abby and Christopher

6

MEET THE FOSTER PARENTS

Loving Homes Needed by Anne Austin
Sooner Catholic April 4, 2004

It is difficult to imagine caring for a family of 13 children. It is even more difficult to imagine that eight of the children are adopted, three are biological and, often there is an infant who is cared for as their foster child. Sometimes there are two foster babies brought into their home. It is staggering to think that the couple caring for this family has, as foster parents, protected, nurtured and loved 151 babies over the past 25 years. The couple is Walter and Ray Ann Merchant and the family is theirs.

"I married a man who let me have my dream of raising all kinds of children in need," said Ray Ann. "He not only allowed me to realize my dream...he made it his dream too."

Walter sometimes does not arrive home from work until 7 p.m. Finding a house full of kids and the needs they have might be difficult for some, but not Walter.

"He is great at taking over with the children, doing baths and pitching in on all the other chores that come with raising a large family."

Ray Ann and Walter feel that they were called to care for these children and infants in need of love before they go to their own homes. The Merchants have a culturally blended family, and Ray Ann feels that the children have grown up without experiencing racism. *"All of our family members, friends, neighbors, schools and our church (Epiphany Catholic Church) have been incredibly supportive and have played a big part in helping us raise our children in a nurturing environment. Foster care brings home the idea that a baby is a baby."*

The work involved in caring for such a huge family doesn't seem to be a concern for Ray Ann. *"It really is true that big families care for each other and take on their own jobs for themselves and to care for the family."*

"One night I woke up realizing that my baby had not woken me for her feeding. When I went into the room to check on her, my 18-year-old twin girls had gotten up to do it."

Ray Ann said that she is a high-energy person and does a workout at 5 a.m. She also has no trouble getting up in the night to tend to a child and then immediately falling back to sleep.

"Walter is always willing to take over if I need extra rest," she said. Needless to say, the Merchant house is always filled with children. Over the recent Spring

Break, not only were there nine of their own children, but three grandsons and many of the children's friends were constantly in the house. "People have said, more than once, that I have a day care," Ray Ann said with a smile.

She has many thoughts to share about being a foster parent. "Being a foster parent is one of the most important things in our lives," she said. "When they put a baby in my arms, I am in awe of God's miracle of life. I am going to be 85 someday and still calling Catholic Charities to please give me a foster child."

Catholic Charities is the adoption agency that the Merchants have chosen to work with in adopting and becoming foster parents. "I am the Director of the North Oklahoma City Birth Choice and I have worked with lots of adoption agencies. Catholic Charities does it right. They minister to moms and are not out for numbers or money. They minister and love the adoptive family and they are there for the foster parents."

"Sometimes, birth moms change their minds on adoption and Catholic Charities never pushes them to go through with the adoption. Working with Catholic Charities over the years, I can say that the staff in Family Support Services is apart from all other adoption agencies," said Ray Ann.

"Some agencies used to say not to bond with the foster babies. Catholic Charities says just the opposite, you have to bond with the babies. Those first few months are the most important in a child's development. That child needs and deserves to be loved. I want to add that

*being a foster parent is not something that just one
spouse should do."*

*There are many circumstances that might bring a
foster child into the Merchant home. Sometimes, a birth
mother may need time before she is willing to place her
child in an adoptive home. Sometimes the decision has
been made, but paper or legal work is not completed
before leaving the hospital.*

*"When our foster babies leave, I send a letter to the
mother asking her to tell the baby that he or she was
very loved. We haven't heard from our foster children,
but there is a man in our parish who was adopted
after he left us. It has been wonderful to see him grow.
I know loving your foster child makes it very hard to
say goodbye... but it should be hard. All of our family
members react in different ways, but we all know that
the babies needed us and we gave them everything
before they went home."*

* * *

Ray Ann, Walter, and their children quickly became
attached to Abby and Christopher. After we learned
about their family and later met them, we knew how
special they were. In our eyes, they were saints!

When Abby and Christopher were just several days
old, Ray brought them to Catholic Charities everyday to
allow us to begin bonding immediately. It was such a
wonderful feeling knowing they were going to be coming
home with us soon.

7

BRINGING CHRISTOPHER AND ABBY HOME

Email Update - 04/6/04
The Babies are Coming!

Dear Friends and Family,

Change of plans...The babies will get to come home with us much sooner than expected. We just got a call today and found out they'll be here Wednesday (<u>tomorrow</u>) morning!

We've been busy borrowing the necessities while waiting for everything to be finalized. We can't wait!

Foster mom says they're outgrowing newborn diapers and infant clothing. She says they sleep five hours a stretch at night, but she has had a lot of experience with babies. We'll see what they do when

*they get over here where it is quiet! (They
are used to a lot of commotion.)*

*Thank you for all of your thoughts
and prayers. Keep 'em coming; we're
almost there!*

*Love,
Valerie, Roger, Abby and Christopher*

What a happy day it was. We were accustomed to Ray
bringing the babies up to Catholic Charities for us to
visit. But the day they went home with us, it was Walter
who brought them. Ray got too attached, as she always
did Walter explained, and had him do the final drop off.
She wrote a letter to us and the twins:

*Dear Valerie,
What a wonderful day this is for you and
your husband. Your little ones are both
so precious, so unique. They each have
their own little personality. He is very
laid back and calm...she on the other
hand wants what she wants and wants
it right now. She likes having her brother
near her.*

*Both Walter and I feel very good
about this placement. We know these
little ones are going exactly where they
need to go. You will be great parents.
Please tell them they were very loved by*

all of us. We have enjoyed having them in our home and they will always have a special place in our hearts. Our son Anthony is especially going to miss the little boy. He is very attached to him.

Along with the babies, we are sending you all our best wishes and our prayers. If we can help in any way, just call. I know you are both going to handle parenting just great. Trust your instincts and remember God knows what He is doing and He put these babies with you for a reason.

Congratulations,
Ray and Walter

8

BABIES DON'T COME WITH MANUALS

So how the heck do you know what to do when they first come home? When you haven't gone to any classes at the hospital, or had the nurse show you what to do the first few times? I couldn't breast feed, and I didn't know how they got those wrappy things so dang tight around their little bitty bodies.

We had so many people bring us wonderful dinners, soft blankets and cute onesies. But one of the best homecoming gifts of all was from my sweet cousin Meredith, a neo-natal nurse. She brought herself, and showed us what to do. She also let us borrow a rocking swing; our lifesaver on many occasions.

Meredith gave swaddling instructions, showed us how to microwave the nipple sterilizer, bring a bottle to the right temperature, and hold our tiny babies. With her gentle teaching, I didn't feel quite so inept. I wanted her to move in, but she had her own family to care for!

For the first month or so, the babies slept swaddled separately, but wedged side-by-side in an old-fashioned white wooden bassinet. It was a gift from my friend Lisa, who had also adopted a darling little girl. She brought it to me the minute I told her the babies were coming home.

Abby and Christopher were so cute smashed together and turned towards one another. They were used to entangling their arms and legs together in the womb. It must have been strange to be in separate burrito blankets, unable to touch each other.

We were afraid to sleep. We were so excited and scared all at the same time. Of course, twins wake up at different times, and they need diapers changed at different times. We were up non-stop. By the time we got back to sleep, it was time to get up again.

The doctor told us to record how much they ate and their diaper status. I was a zombie and couldn't remember which child I had fed, how much and at what time. I needed a schedule. I needed a list on an Excel spreadsheet.

My friend Karen died laughing when she came to visit and saw my red binder and spreadsheet showing dates, times, feedings in amounts, and when each baby had a poopy diaper. Well, how else was a sleep-deprived mom supposed to keep track? I look back now and can't believe I did it either. But at the time, it helped keep me sane. Roger and I couldn't continue at this pace. I think we both played possum and pretended to be asleep so the other would get up when the babies cried. We eventually came up with a plan.

Both of us got up to feed the babies every few hours. But if there was crying in between, we took turns getting up every other night. It at least gave one of us a little more sleep. We were having such a hard time with the pace of twins; we couldn't imagine either Nicole or the birth father on their own.

Email Update - 04/11/04

Hello Friends!

Even though I haven't talked to you in a while, we have very exciting news. I wanted you to know that our Christmas card photo will have two additional family members! We are adopting twins.

We are still in the middle of the process, but are caring for the twins until everything is resolved. Their names are Christopher and Abby, and they are adorable. This is the most fun we have ever had, (and we are busy, exhausted, sore, and hungry, too...as you all can relate!) Keep us in your prayers that everything works out.

Love,
Valerie, Roger, Abby and Christopher

Email Update - 04/17/04

Dear Friends and Family,

It's been a week so far and we're still alive and still awake! They are doing great and growing bigger every day. It looks like the court date may drag on several months, so we are glad that we have them early, so we can bond and get to know them.

Thank you all for your thoughts, prayers, food, diapers and formula!

Love,
Valerie, Roger, Abby and Christopher

9

THE BLOW WE DIDN'T SEE COMING

After being off for more than three months, going back to work was surreal. It was so nice to have a break and distraction from everything going on at home. It almost felt like vacation to interact with adults and to go out for lunch.

Eating had been a challenge. I couldn't seem to satisfy my hunger at home, because I never had time to eat more than a bite of something here or there, usually cold. I had begun to wonder how hot food tasted, and I wasn't even breast-feeding. And forget about Roger and I eating a meal at the same time.

Then, the very day we went back to reality and work, we were punched in the stomach. On the front page of the *The Oklahoman* was an article about the birth father telling his side of the story. Imagine finding out for the first time that the Choctaw Nation was not approving us as prospective adoptive parents. We had thought their approval was just a formality, something Catholic Charities had to follow, and had not spent any time considering the tribe's involvement.

Law Working to Preserve Kids' Indian Heritage
by Judy Gibbs Robinson
The Oklahoman July 6, 2004

A bassinet filled with baby clothes rests at the end of Jimmy Dwayne Williams' bed in his parent's home. The 23-year-old unemployed laborer hopes to fill it soon with his infant twins, born in March to a girlfriend who put them up for adoption. The babies are nearly four months old. Jimmy has yet to see them, although he has refused steadfastly to relinquish his parental rights. "I don't even have a picture," he said.

Williams' plight is a common one for young American Indian fathers, said John Roberts, a lawyer representing the Choctaw Nation in the custody case. Despite protections in the federal Indian Child Welfare Act, Indian men often have to go to court to fight for custody of their children, he said. "I travel all over Oklahoma and litigate these cases," Roberts said.

With the third-largest Indian population in the country, Oklahoma is fertile ground for Indian Child Welfare Act cases. In an article this year in the Oklahoma Bar Journal, Carter County District Judge Tom Walker advised lawyers to study the act if they haven't already. "Failing to do so is a jurisdictional disaster waiting to happen," he wrote.

Nationally, about 1.6 percent of Indian children are in non-parental placement, said Steve Hager, managing attorney for Oklahoma Indian Legal Services. He said the Indian Child Welfare Act should come into play in every one of those custody cases, but it doesn't always. "Whenever I speak at conferences, I always say there are three classifications of lawyers in Oklahoma: Those who have had an ICWA case, those who will have one, and those who had one but didn't know it," he said.

Failure to invoke the act continues to drain Oklahoma tribes of their children. Kara Whitworth, program manager for child welfare with the Cherokee Nation, estimates 12 Cherokee children a year are placed in foster or adoptive homes without the tribe's knowledge. "I would say there's probably a new case a month where someone forgot to give us notice. We may hear about it a year later," she said.

Roberts said the losses hurt. "Some are kids who need to be taken away from their parents, don't get me wrong. But that's the tribe's most vital resource. That's their future."

Indian Children, Indian Families

Protecting that resource was one of the goals when Congress passed the Indian Child Welfare Act in 1978.

A 1974 study found 25 percent to 35 percent of Indian children had been removed from their families at some point in their lives. "There are still a disproportionate number of Indian children in foster care," said B.J. Jones, author of a handbook on the Indian Child Welfare Act published by the American Bar Association. "At least now they're in Indian homes or homes the tribes approved of."

Keeping Indian children in Indian homes is vital for the tribes and for the children, who need to grow up connected to the past, Jones said in a telephone interview from the Northern Plains Tribal Judicial Training Institute, where he is Director. He thinks many problems in Indian families today can be traced to former U.S. policies removing Indian children from traditional homes and sending them to boarding schools where they lost their languages and cultures.

That policy "created generations of Indian people who, when they grew up, didn't know what it meant to be Indian," Jones said. "It's almost like a cultural detachment disorder. They don't know who they are."

Often they do not know how to parent, either, Hager said. "People kind of cringe when I say this, but basically, the U.S. government has tried ... to destroy this culture," Hager said. "They've worked very hard to make sure Indian families are sort of left behind, and we're still seeing the results of that."

Possible Shortcomings

The law has doubtless slowed the flow of children from their tribes, but Walker, who is Cherokee and Wyandotte, wonders whether it was too little, too late. "The act is designed to preserve tribal culture. In many areas of the United States, that culture has been lost. It's just gone," he said.

While Walker likes the Indian Child Welfare Act, he said it has made family law more convoluted. And he questions whether it always serves the child best.

"I can see where we've made progress," said Whitworth, the Cherokee Nation's program manager. "I can also see where it's a continual learning process."

Jones said people are becoming impatient because Indian families are still not flourishing; a generation after the Indian Child Welfare Act took effect. "You're not going to see the dramatic change in one generation. It may even take seven generations," he said.

Even if he does not win custody, Jimmy Williams' babies will grow up Choctaw because Catholic Charities, the adoption agency involved, placed them with another Choctaw family.

The Choctaw Nation refuses to accept that placement, siding instead with Williams and his parents. In a motion filed in the case May 14, Roberts wrote that the Indian Child Welfare Act gave the tribe, not the adoption agency, the right to choose. "It is clear that an Indian child must be placed, in the absence of good cause, with a member of the Indian child's extended family," Roberts wrote.

The babies' birth mother could not be reached for comment. Speaking on her behalf, her mother declined to comment, noting it was a private matter.

Catholic Charities also cited confidentiality in

declining to comment on the case. But Family Support Director Julia Reed said the Indian Child Welfare Act comes into play often in adoption cases the agency handles. "We work hard to abide by the Indian Child Welfare Act. We understand the procedures involved, and we really work hard to do the right thing for the child in the context of the law," Reed said.

She said the law makes exceptions when there are "compelling reasons" why a baby should not be placed with the immediate family. "No matter what side you're on, there's emotional involvement and emotional pain. We would not say we had a compelling reason unless we thought the proof was available to us," she said.

Williams seems baffled by the proceedings. To him, what is right seems clear: "It seems to me if the mother doesn't want the kids, the father should be able to go to the hospital and get them," he said.

* * *

At the time, Catholic Charities believed that the Indian Child Welfare Act (ICWA) rules, (which we were not familiar with) had been followed, and the tribe was not going to disapprove us. Roger was Choctaw, and they knew of the birth father's family drug history.

If the newspaper story wasn't enough for one day, we were also called by Catholic Charities to advise us for the first time, that we would have to bring Christopher and Abby to Catholic Charities for a visitation with the birth father. We were quite shell-shocked, never dreaming this could be a possibility.

After speaking with an attorney friend about the prospect of this visitation, she advised against it until after the next hearing unless it was court ordered. Catholic Charities said we didn't have a choice, and confirmed the court order. I asked for a copy of the order. I was sick to my stomach at the thought of enduring the birth father being with them, and even sicker when I found out that the court order included the birth father's parents and grandparents. The visit would last at least two hours.

Please, God, don't put us through this. We were especially anxious, because up to this point, we had been waiting for the process to be over. The birth father had not seen us, and did not know our name. Or, so we thought. We later found out that the tribe's attorney had said our name in court.

We felt our privacy had been violated, and the safety of the children compromised. Whatever happened to our desire for a private, closed adoption? Things were really getting messy and felt out of our control. Now we would be placing Christopher and Abby in the hands of the birth father's family.

I tried to find that quiet place to let God speak to my heart.... Trust in Me, my child. Don't I always take care of you? I will get you through your pain and uncertainty. Luckily, a stranger felt the same way we did, and wrote a letter to the editor of the The Oklahoman.

Adoption Law's Intent Ignored by Paige Lee
The Oklahoman July 21, 2004

I am an attorney practicing in the Oklahoma County District Court with eight years of experience representing birth mothers in adoption proceedings. I've handled numerous adoptions on behalf of birth mothers where the applicability of the Indian Child Welfare Act (ICWA) was at issue.

"Law Working to Preserve Kids' Indian Heritage" (feature, July 6) failed to address the important doctrine of "existing Indian family." This doctrine is, in essence, summed up by the comment B. J. Jones made in the article: "Keeping Indian children in Indian homes is vital for the tribes and for the children who need to grow up connected to the past."

The intent of the ICWA was always to prevent the removal of Indian children from existing Indian families; families, who practice tribal cultures, are living on reservations, are active politically, etc. It was never the intent of the act to take a child with Indian blood, often regardless of the amount, and attribute to that child the status of "Indian" even if, should the birth mother keep the child, there would be no Indian culture in that child's life.

The article failed to address whether the birth mother was herself Indian... Often she is not. In this instance, the respective Indian tribe attempts to circumvent her right to choose the appropriate home for the child and orders her to place with an Indian family.

Yes, the rights of the tribe trump the rights of the woman who carried the child and gave birth to him, even if her only tie to Indian heritage is her one-time relationship with the birth father.

As to Jimmy Dwayne Williams' statement that if the mother doesn't want the children, he should have them, the law allows that to happen. Regardless of his status as an Indian, Williams could have protected his rights to the children simply by supporting the woman he impregnated.

Had he bought her maternity clothes, furnished support or paid medical bills for her, he would have a constitutionally protected right to raise those children, even if the mother doesn't want to. There is no information in the story as to whether Williams did these things. If he didn't, his failure to do so ensured that most likely, his consent to the adoption is not necessary...

The legal intent behind such a requirement comes all the way from the United States Supreme Court: "If a father won't support the mother of his child during her pregnancy, the law should not require her to consult him on decisions regarding the child since he can't be counted on to maintain support for the child for the next 18 years."

10

VISITATION

Preoccupied with the prospect of visitation, after reading the article and seeing the birth father's photo for the first time made everything worse. *What if the family saw us at the visitation and found out where we lived? What if they followed us home?*

We were in this for a closed adoption, not open and public. But with the newspaper article, all that changed. We spent the next few days preparing ourselves emotionally and mentally for the visit, knowing that the babies would be sensing our anxiety. Nothing can prepare you for the reality.

We all went to the meeting in separate cars, at different times to make sure we were not seen, nor could be followed. I even had my friend Rene act as a decoy and take the kids in a separate entrance so they wouldn't know our car. It felt creepy. Everyone arrived early. They didn't just bring the court ordered five people, the birth father brought his extended family; aunts, uncles, cousins, grandparents, parents and friends.

In addition to this large group, Catholic Charities had a plain-clothes police officer there, just in case. We later learned the officer was working as a favor because she was an adoptive parent through Catholic Charities as well.

We protested that so many people were there, as we were told the court order had specified just five people. And, after we poked around, we were livid to find out there was no actual court order. However, Catholic Charities would not take sides with the birth mother, the birth father or us. So we were left with no choice but to follow through. During all of the waiting and going back and forth to determine if the court order existed and who was allowed to visit, Christopher and Abby sensed our anxiety and became upset.

Luckily, the police officer saw what was happening and only allowed two people to visit Christopher and Abby at a time. Roger and I, having come in a back door with the kids, waited in an office as Sabra pried them away from us to meet the birth father's family. I remember a feeling of dread, followed by anger, then fear.

Not ten minutes into the visit, all we could hear were the babies screaming and crying, non-stop.

I wanted to burst into the room and hold them and soothe them. Sabra, with her soothing spirit, stepped up and did it for us. She brought them back to us, one-by-one, to calm them. After they had stopped crying, she would then take them back to the visitation room. This went on for what felt like eternity, back and forth. It was the longest forty-five minutes of my life.

Then, Sabra returned and told us the visit was over. *After only forty-five minutes? What happened? They brought all of those people to see the children they were fighting for, and they did not take the full two hours to see them?*

When Sabra put Abby back in to my arms, I had never seen her so upset. She sobbed so hard, unable to catch her breath, until she fell asleep in my arms. We also learned that the birth father had spent less than ten total minutes out of the allowed two hours in the room during the visit.

The police officer said the main topic of conversation between family members was not about the babies, but about going to eat at Catfish Cabin after the visit. *They left because they were hungry.*

11

THE WORST DAY OF OUR LIVES

Today was a big day in court. I waited anxiously at home with the babies to hear how the ruling regarding termination of the birth father's parental rights would be decided. The birth father had not paid any support to Nicole during her pregnancy. State law states a biological parent must grasp his parental rights, no matter where the children are located, and pay a reasonable amount of support during the pregnancy. And, Catholic Charities had never seen a birth father show or pay such little support without having his rights terminated.

If the ruling was in our favor, and Catholic Charities was able to get the birth father's parental rights terminated, it would allow us to finalize the adoption and the babies would be legally ours. I called Sabra constantly to see if court was out. Because the hearing was between Catholic Charities and the birth father, we did not attend the court hearing in person.

While we waited, Roger took our last, geriatric furry child, Gabby, to the vet to be put to rest. Before Christopher and Abby, we felt like we ran an assisted living center for four-legged senior citizens. We had lost Wylie, our eighteen-year-old mini Sheltie, and Asti, my fourteen-year-old cocker spaniel, the year before.

Later during the afternoon feeding, Grandma Muzzie and Grandpa Leroy stopped by for a visit and marveled at how big Christopher and Abby were growing. We also had frequent visits from friends and neighbors dropping off food and gifts, or just wanting to sneak a peek at the infamous new twins in our lives.

We weren't surprised to hear an unexpected knock at the door. Sabra had stopped by, as she often did. But this time she had Alma, another Catholic Charities social worker with her. *This can't be good.* I showed her into the den. She asked where Roger was, and I explained about Gabby. I introduced her to my parents and she peeked in on the babies.

"Valerie, we have come to tell you that you lost," she said.

We lost? Lost what? What did that mean?

"The birth father won. His parental rights can't be terminated. Nicole has decided to go ahead and take the babies back and raise them herself so he won't have them all of the time. There is nothing you can do."

"Nicole knows it will be hard for you to say goodbye, so she is going to let you keep them another week before you have to return them, " Sabra continued.

What was this? It sounded like we are talking

about an overdue library book or Blockbuster movie.

I was stunned. This could not be happening. These were our babies. We had named them, lost countless hours of sleep over them, bonded with them, and loved them for over five months.

I lost it. I saw Roger pulling into the driveway, less one fluffy fourteen year-old American Eskimo, and I ran outside to his car door, sobbing, not even letting him get out. He saw the unfamiliar cars in our driveway, my tears, and my pain. Although in his own pain from watching Gabby move from this earth to doggie heaven within the last half hour, he knew immediately what had happened.

We held each other and I couldn't catch my breath from sobbing, just as Abby had done a few weeks before. We walked back inside and Sabra explained again that the judge had ruled in the birth father's favor. The judge had decided that the birth father had grasped his parental rights during Nicole's pregnancy when the birth father's mother paid for 'maternity clothes', and gave Nicole a Christmas card with a check for fifty dollars.

That was it. *That's all you have to do to grasp your rights? That was considered 'commensurate with your ability to pay?'*

"There must be something we can do," Roger said. "Appeal? Fight? Get our own attorney?"

"No, according to the Catholic Charities attorney, there is nothing you can do," Sabra said as she watched the pain we were going through.

We were devastated. Catholic Charities had said

there was such a slim chance the birth father would win. If they hadn't been so confident of the court's ability to terminate the birth father's parental rights, they never would have placed Christopher and Abby in our care before the outcome of the hearing. But they were so sure that it would be finalized, they had allowed it. Now here we were facing the worst day of our lives.

Roger asked if we could call Nicole and her parents to see if we could get our own attorney and try to fight. Thank goodness, Sabra said yes to this idea. Roger and I left the room. He wrapped me in his arms, assuring me over and over that we would 'not let them take our babies.'

It was very hard for me to pray 'Thy will be done' on this very night, when in my mind there was only one right answer. I prayed it anyway.

I didn't express it to Roger, but I was trying to prepare myself that God knew what He was doing. If it really was His will to take these children from our home and place them back with Nicole, there was a reason we had had them, if only for a short time. I just had to believe that God would give me the strength to face this obstacle, because I certainly couldn't do it without Him.

All along Roger had said we wouldn't let this happen; we would fight. 'Never quit, never give in, and never surrender.' I knew he was just trying to make me feel better. But Sabra's words kept echoing in my head... *I'm so sorry; there is nothing you can do.*

Before I drifted off to sleep, I took time to listen in silence. *....do not let fear rule your heart and your* *life. You cannot control all circumstances around you. Accept the things that God puts in your life as gifts from Him. Enjoy and appreciate how he chooses to show his work. Know that He will never let you down, or let you suffer. Has He ever failed to provide for your needs? Let Him do His job and quit trying to do it for Him. He knows what is best for you. You need only to slow down and take the time to listen to His voice. Not others, but the One who knows you best. Your Father and Savior. He knows you are hurting right now. He wants you to lean on and trust in Him. He is preparing you for things greater than you can imagine and He needs you quiet and still. Slow down. Rest in his peaceful arms, open your heart and soul to Him, and His will. He will provide, as always. He loves you very much. Feel His love and presence around you.*

And somehow, emotionally and physically drained, I slept through the night.

Email Update - 08/17/04

Dear Friends and Family,
Yesterday was a long day, and unfortunately, things did not go the way we had hoped and anticipated. The judge ruled in favor of the birth father, because he had given $139 worth of gifts and had made two phone calls to the birth mother during her pregnancy. It did not matter in court that he used drugs. What was

in the best interest of the babies was not
discussed.

   The next step is that the birth mother
will rescind her relinquishment of her
rights, and take the babies back. But
then, she will have to give the birth father
visitation. We plan to talk to an attorney
to see what, if anything, we can do. In the
meantime, the babies laugh and smile, not
knowing how drastically their little lives
are going to change soon. We know that
within the week they may be gone forever.

   But we are in this for the long haul
and will fight as hard as possible, while
doing what the birth mother wants us to.
She is as devastated as we are. She had
already moved things to her new dorm
room and met her new college roommate.
We know that no matter what happens,
these have been the most fun and
rewarding five months of our lives. Keep
the prayers coming, this is the hard part!

Love,
Valerie, Roger, Abby and Christopher

12

THE BATTLE BEGINS

Roger was my rock and he said we would fight. But if we lost in court and Catholic Charities would not fight for us, how could Roger promise me we would fight and keep the kids? I knew I was a woman of faith. Maybe in the past I had given in or up too easily; chalking things up to God's will. I was praying again with conditions and felt this was God's way of making it difficult. But I knew He would give me the strength to deal with whatever the end result would be.

Friends didn't know what to say. Even Catholic Charities said, "There are other babies. We will put you on the top of the list." *How could Catholic Charities give up on us so easily? How could there be no options?*

I had recently gone through a leadership program that threw me together with forty of our city's leaders in various capacities. One of them was feisty County Judge Hinton. I called Judge Hinton to tell her about our situation, and to see if she could give me any direction. She was off work that day, but they gave me her cell phone number. I called; no answer. I left a long-winded, desperate message pleading for any guidance. It seemed like an eternity before she called me back.

In the meantime, I didn't go into work that day. I was a basket case. I called my friend Sharon, who has one of the biggest hearts I know. Her way of showing 'Mama Bear' comfort was taking me, swollen eyes and all, to a nice restaurant for good comfort food. I didn't want to leave the house, but the babies were napping, the nanny was available, and I was starving in a house with an empty fridge. *Who had time to go to the grocery store now?*

My memory was shot on many things, but this is so clear in my head; a day I will never forget. The delicious flavors of the food still linger. We went to Rococo; a quaint local restaurant that served handmade pasta. My favorite is linguini with pesto. No one in this town makes a better pesto. Other restaurants always adulterate it with heavy cream or too much olive oil, losing the flavor that my taste buds recall from trips to Italy. However, Rococo nails it.

Like many other things, including organizing, labeling things, and making lists, food was another one of those things that could take my mind elsewhere. At that moment, I felt like I had control. Midway through my meal, as that linguini went into my mouth like the big hug of a comforting friend, my cell phone rang.

It was Judge Hinton. I about choked. What if

she told me there was no hope and no place to turn? I dropped my fork, grabbed my phone and ran outside to take the call.

"I got your voice mail. There are many things you can do. You have a lot of options," she said matter-of-factly.

"We have options? What kind of options?" Was I hearing her correctly? She was talking so fast I couldn't process it all. My heart and brain were trying to keep up, but her words 'you have options' kept replaying in my mind. *Options. Not black or white. Multiple choices!*

I came back to the conversation to hear her say that it was up to us to find a good attorney that knew a lot about the Indian Child Welfare Act, and then find out what we could do to get in the fight. We were now considered an 'interested party', and we were more than interested. It was one of hundreds of new legal terms I was about to learn over the next several years.

My linguine was cold, but at this point, I was so excited I didn't care. My tears had dried up and were replaced with hope.

"What do you want for dessert?" Sharon asked. She was my eat-dessert-first friend that knew me so well. The warm hazelnut flourless chocolate cake was euphoria on a fork. Food never tasted so good.

13

A NEW ME

I thought the four little words 'Thy Will Be Done' changed my life. However, I put those words with 'You Have Options', and I was a new woman. A force to be reckoned with. I have never felt so empowered in my life.

I think at that moment, I understood Roger and how he had already felt a strong force. Until this point in my life, I had never faced any real adversity in my life, or had been one to rock the boat very much. I was a people pleaser and a rule follower; a good corporate employee. But things were about to change for me, and in a good way. You don't feel it in your core until you have something deeply worth fighting for.

Roger was glad I had called Judge Hinton for direction, but he hadn't doubted things in the first place. As an entrepreneur, he has had many seemingly insurmountable obstacles to overcome, professionally and personally. Nothing had been too great. He has great admiration for Winston Churchill and can recite parts of his speeches. Roger's combined 'Never Quit, Never Give In, Never Surrender' paraphrase kept me going as I often repeated my own version in my head, 'Never Give Up, Never Give In.'

14

A NEW HOBBY

Christopher and Abby were good sleepers. Since they were born, I had read and followed to a 'T', a book called *On Becoming Baby Wise*. It was right up my alley. You put the kids on a strict schedule for eating and sleeping. The hard part was that initially you had to endure the several nights of their crying forever in their cribs and not feeding them on demand. Luckily, it didn't take that long, and the results were beautiful.

Beginning when they were three months old, they slept through the night, rarely awakening. They went down at 6:30 p.m., and woke up at 6:30 a.m. This meant Roger and I had some semblance of a life after they went to bed. We could enjoy a home-cooked meal, then resume working on to our new favorite pastime—detective work and legal research.

Roger loved the investigative work and I loved the legal research part. Instead of reading how-to books on parenting, I felt I had become a law student overnight as I took case law and state and federal adoption statutes to bed. But I had much more motivation to get the answers right than to just pass a class or the bar exam. This was real life, and two precious children's lives were in the balance.

Roger and I became very familiar with all of the court websites where you can snoop around reading court cases and transcripts of unsealed documents. It was both enlightening and productive.

Roger proved to be quite the Sherlock Holmes, minus the bloodhound and pipe. He was always coming up with obscure details and finding out pertinent information when we needed it. Let's just say that throughout this whole journey, the babies were not the only things that fell in our laps. A police report found its way to us, and as we read it, we were amazed.

The birth father was first arrested as a minor for speeding and hitting a car. He was charged with leaving the scene of an auto accident, possession of marijuana and drug paraphernalia, including scales and a pipe. He was able to plea it down to Disorderly Conduct and paid a minor fine. We began to see a pattern of lapsed judgment after reading about his second arrest on drug related charges.

We stumbled upon the document showing that the birth father's mother had filed a Victim's Protective Order against her husband. While separated, he had hit her in front of their minor child when he came to get a gun out of the house. We now had something important to help our case for custody.

During this time, my faith deepened as Roger and I prayed every night for God's direction and will. And, every time we felt that adrenaline rush from stumbling upon something that would help our case. It felt like God's gentle guidance opening our spirits for direction.

I often thought of the huge painted icon of Mary holding Jesus as a small child in our Church. It is the centerpiece. Since most of our service is not in English, I took time to pray and reflect, often just staring into the huge, soulful eyes of Mary.

I'd always had a strong connection with Mary, (Mother of God, or as she is called in our church, the Theotokos), but never so much as then. Looking at her and thinking of what we were going through and the prospect of losing our children was nothing compared to watching your son be humiliated, bullied, whipped, spat at and crucified on the cross.

She became my intercessor. I still prayed to Jesus, but who better to ask Jesus for the protection of our children than his Mother? I just felt like she had an 'in', a home court advantage. Wouldn't the Mother of God know what a mom was going though? At least she could put in a good word or two.

15

IN THE FIGHT

Technically, we now had a 'Failed Adoption.' We were running out of the time before Nicole would come to take back Christopher and Abby. The first attorney we contacted was helpful, but decided our case was too specialized for him. He recommended Noel Tucker, a razor sharp adoption attorney who was better versed in Indian cases. She had also taught continuing education on ICWA topic for the Bar Association.

We met with Noel and hired her immediately. She was tough as nails and knew her stuff. It was obvious to us that her job was her passion. She and her husband practiced together in an unpretentious office space tucked in an old, historic building on Main Street in Edmond, Oklahoma.

Noel immediately filed a motion to intervene since the children had been in our care essentially since birth, and we became an 'interested party'. If we didn't step in at this point, custody may be granted to the birth father without the court hearing about the birth father's drug use, and without consideration of the best interest of the children. Noel said we should appeal the judge's decision to the Catholic Charities case between the birth father and birth mother. She also said our chances were very slim. *She gave us a five percent chance, but just last week the odds were even worse. Zero percent. Five percent sounded pretty great to me.*

Though many in our shoes might have disagreed, we trusted Noel's opinion that our case was worthy of an Appeal, even though it would be difficult to overturn. She constantly reminded us that the adoption process would be detailed and complicated. She also taught us that along the path to our adoption, there would be many rabbit trails to follow, each with their own set of consequences. However, she felt confident she could keep the failed adoption case alive through an Appeal, as well as exploring best interest of the child, custody and guardianship options if the Appeal failed.

"Let's do it," Roger said. We knew we had a long road ahead of us, but we were never giving up, never giving in, and never surrendering. After talking with Catholic Charities and letting them know that we did have options and were going to exercise them, we asked if they would join us in the appeal.

It would be a long, expensive shot. Catholic Charities had never had a case like this, and were reluctant to fight as they were a non-profit agency with limited resources. However, we offered to champion the cause with Noel leading the case, and they eventually came onboard with us.

In the meantime, Sabra called Nicole and told her it was best to leave Abby and Christopher with us until we heard the outcome of our Appeal. All parties agreed, and we were granted a temporary reprieve. Maybe I could get some sleep for a night without the worry of 'only a few more nights with the babies', temporarily lifted. But future nights of peaceful sleep would prove to be rare for many years.

We weren't just fighting to keep Christopher and Abby out of the care of the birth father. We were up against every member of his family, and the Choctaw Nation. In district court, when there is no Indian blood involved, you don't have such a high standard of law to follow as when the Indian Child Welfare Act is in place.

The Federal Law imposes a Placement Preference, which says that the tribe prefers the children to be placed in a certain order. In any adoptive placement of an Indian child, as codified under State Law, a preference shall be given, in the absence of good cause to the contrary, to a placement with:

- A member of the child's extended family
- Other members of the Indian child's tribe
- Other Indian families

We were number three on the list. So we needed to eliminate numbers one and two, and show there was cause to the contrary for placing the children in an unsafe environment with the biological extended family.

It sounded simple enough. But in reality, eliminating placement meant proving the birth father, his parents, and any other interested blood relative were unsuitable to adopt the children. This put us much farther down on the Placement Preference list.

16

THE DAY WE MET
THE CHIEF

Journal - 10/04/04

Today we vacillated about going to the Choctaw Nation meeting where the Chief was to speak in favor of gaming legislation. But as I was showering, I had a very loud and clear thought that we should go.

Roger felt that since the tribe had not responded to our repeated attempts to talk or schedule a meeting with the Chief, that there was no hope in garnering their support, even though Roger is a member of the tribe.

I have felt that until they tell us where they stand, (rather than reading about it in the newspaper) we should continue to pursue them.

This is the first time Roger and I disagreed on how to approach this, but I was adamant. Roger eventually conceded that it wouldn't hurt to go. In my mind, how else would we get in front of the Chief? Besides, it was at my alma mater, The University of Oklahoma, and only thirty minutes away.

We bundled up Abby and Christopher, all of their gear required to leave the house for more than two hours, and took them to Norman, Oklahoma. There were only about one hundred people there, and we sat in the back row.

The tribe talked about their many accomplishments, what they had done for their members and what State Question 712 could do for tribal gaming. The tribe really had come a long way, especially under this Chief.

Chief Pyle seemed to be a very good man. I felt anxious and excited for him to stop talking and hoped he wouldn't have handlers that would whisk him quickly away from the crowds. As he was winding down and the meeting was over, we made a beeline for Chief Pyle.

There were a few people ahead of us, but I pushed through before he could get away. How could he resist a photo-op with such cute babies? Since we had called him over the last few months to the point of making a nuisance of ourselves, as well as the barrage of the letter writing campaign we orchestrated to get his attention, it only took a couple of seconds after we introduced ourselves for the Chief to recognize our names.

The Chief motioned for the photographer to take our picture with him for the tribe's newspaper. I knew then we had established a little rapport. He was so approachable and we had his attention.

I quickly gave him the bullet points I had rehearsed in the shower. "The tribe is making such inroads on eradicating drug use, why would the tribe want to get involved and support a known drug user and place these children in his hands?" I asked.

The Chief was gracious and listened to me talk on and on about who we were and why we needed his help. I wanted him to know we had a loving, Choctaw home, and we were willing to show the children their Indian heritage, just as the paper had discussed concerns about adoption placements outside of the tribe. He told us he was so glad we had introduced ourselves, and said he would put us in capable hands.

He then introduced us to Nathan Miller, the Director of the Choctaw Nation's Family Services Division.

We gave Mr. Miller the same bullet points we had just given the Chief. He recognized our case, saying he had received the file on Friday, but hadn't yet read it all. He said he would finish it, and we could call him on Monday of the next week. Mr. Miller added that because we were Choctaw, if the birth father had drug problems and the grandparents weren't suitable, we could be considered as prospective adoptive parents.

Mr. Miller watched us as we held the kids and commented that we had obviously bonded with Abby and Christopher. When we questioned him about the tribe's attorney making light of the father's drug use in the newspaper, he said that the attorney was 'just our outside lawyer,' as if the comments didn't have much credence. Mr. Miller was very kind, and assured us that he would read everything and that the tribe wanted to not only make sure the ICWA was followed, but also that the children's bests interests were looked after. It all sounded logical and reasonable.

We were very hopeful after our meeting. We then met the Assistant Chief, who was also familiar with our situation. The Assistant Chief also told us to contact him if we needed anything. I am so glad we came today!!!

17

MEETING WITH THE TRIBE

After having met with the tribe's Director of Family Services at the University of Oklahoma meeting, we scheduled a time to drive to Durant, Oklahoma and discuss our situation with the tribe. I couldn't sleep the night before the meeting from sheer excitement and anticipation that this nightmare would be over soon. Surely, we could convince them that we were the best home for Christopher and Abby.

Roger and I made the three-hour drive to Durant. Again, Nathan Miller, the Director met us and greeted us warmly. I tried to let Roger talk, but I couldn't help myself and jumped in to give my 'pitch.'

I told him, "We were more than a little surprised that the tribe came out supporting the birth father, knowing he had drug issues, without giving us a chance to talk to you."

"We didn't come out supporting the birth father," Mr. Miller said.

Had I hear him correctly? "Yes, yes you did," I said. "The transcript here says that the lawyer was there representing the Choctaw Nation and the birth father. (I had a copy of the transcript from the initial paternity case that we were not involved in when Catholic Charities was trying to terminate the birth father's rights.) It was also written in an article about the ICWA on the front page of the *The Oklahoman* newspaper, and stated that the Choctaw Nation was refusing to accept our placement and were siding with the birth father and his parents."

"Well, we didn't send a lawyer to court saying that."

"You didn't? Isn't he your lawyer?"

"No, he is not. His father is our outside lawyer, but we hadn't met with him and discussed who we were going to support."

I was not sure I was grasping this. *They didn't send their lawyer to say the tribe was supporting the birth father? It was our impression the judge had made his decision based mainly upon the tribe's support of the birth father! So, if the tribe had not yet decided to support the birth father, then we assumed the decision made by the judge was based upon the tribe's support of the birth father, which was incorrect information!*

If the tribe's lawyer would just tell the judge this, or schedule a rehearing to say he was not supporting the birth father but supporting us, or even that he was neutral and not supporting either party, this might change the decision.

We were so excited. The meeting only got better. We had done our own investigative work and showed the copies of prior court testimony regarding the birth father's drug use and proof of criminal associations.

Mr. Miller said, "Yes, I am concerned with the birth father, but not as much as I am with his parents."

We were a little surprised, and told him that we had discovered the VPO documenting that the paternal birth grandfather had hit the grandmother in front of a child. However, they were now back together, and we had found nothing else on record.

"They check out real clean," he said. "But," he added, "we have over six pages of concerning information, especially regarding the grandmother." He patted the manila folder on his desk.

I was dying to know what was in there. The tribe must have their own investigators and Nathan Miller must have had some other connections. Mr. Miller then said he had talked to the Chief, and the tribe could not support the grandparents getting the twins.

What about the rest of the family? Mr. Miller wouldn't say, but thought the kids were fine where they were, and he would not have the tribe exert the ICWA Placement Preference. This had already been ruled on in court in favor of the birth father by the mystery lawyer. *Great, our job is done here, I thought. Let's tell all of this to the judge and it will be over.* Apparently, this was all just a misunderstanding and I was so relieved.

Nathan Miller was so kind; he told us about his own children and acknowledged how hard this must be for us to go through.

He gave us supporting case law where a similar situation had happened in another state, and felt our strength was the fact we had bonded with the children for over eight months. He told us we would be acceptable adoptive parents since Roger was a member of the Choctaw Nation.

Mr. Miller told us he would set up a meeting with their senior outside lawyer to clear up this mess the following morning. Once again, I was so naïve.

18

STUCK IN THE MUD

Journal - 10/11/04

Still waiting to talk to the tribe to see how Director Nathan Miller's meeting went yesterday. I think this puts the tribe in a very precarious position.

Roger says the tribe hates bad press. Noel says we can request that the tribe's lawyer's son be removed from the case, based upon our testimony with a letter from the tribe. We will wait a few days to see how they react.

So, doesn't this make it all go away? Can't they just rehear it, throw out the decision and start over since we believe the decision was made on a false assumption?

No meeting happened with the Chief. We were told
that the tribe's lawyer had to cancel the meeting, and
we didn't even know he was going to be in attendance.
We had thought it would only be the Chief and Nathan
Miller.

Journal - 10/26/04

*A Custody Hearing was scheduled for
today in front of our judge. Our attorney,
Noel, as well as the attorney for Catholic
Charities, the birth mother's attorney, and
the birth father's attorney were all there.
A state court-appointed attorney for Abby
and Christopher was also present.*

*We requested a continuance, which
was granted, since we had just hired Noel.
Although we were ready to get this over
with as soon as possible because each
delay was an emotional roller coaster,
every continuance buys us another day
of bonding with Christopher and Abby.*

*In the meantime, the Choctaw Nation
sent a lady from the Family Services
division along with their outside lawyer.
They both are in support of the birth
father and his parents. They continue to
state ICWA violations of notifications, of
which we were all unaware, but which*

should not come in to play.

At this point, it still does not appear that guidance has been given to the outside lawyer regarding who the tribe wants to support-- us or the birth father.

Visitation was court ordered for two hours, twice per week at Catholic Charities until December 7.

I am dreading this. All of the attorneys involved agreed that our attorney, Noel, would prepare for the December Custody Hearing using arguments from the birth father's prior testimony and deposition; where he had lied in court about many things, including drug use.

All of this documentation was collected from the previous court testimony (before we became involved) after the babies were born and after Catholic Charities lost the case to terminate the birth father's parental rights.

Sabra will set up the visitations. The attorney for Catholic Charities will file the Petition in Error (the Appeal), then file a Stay in the Custody Hearing, which means we are requesting that the court does not pursue the Custody Hearing until a decision can be made on our Appeal.

If we win our Appeal, we won't need the Custody Hearing, and it buys more time with the kids.

It is our assignment from the legal team to contact the tribe to see if they have taken a position and request either their being neutral or agreeing to support us on the issue to Stay the Custody Hearing, and possibly agree to a Rehearing.

At this point, we have not received any financial support from the birth father, nor has Nicole, the attorneys, the court, etc. The prior case, which Catholic Charities led and in which we were not a party, was based upon a statute where the birth father did not pay any support to Nicole or the children prior to the children being born. If this continues until December 4, 2004, we will have an opportunity to file a Petition to Terminate Parental Rights of the birth father. We might be able to terminate his parental rights just because he will not give one red cent to support the kids, as is his obligation and the law in our state. This will be a new statute under which we can argue.

This is one of the rabbit trails Noel described. We have many options, including custody without adoption *and to preclude or prohibit the birth grandparents from getting custody, we have the VPO (Victim's Protective Order) against them.*

19

HEARINGS

Email Update - 11/30/04

Dear Friends and Family,
Abby and Christopher continue to thrive.
They are both crawling quickly all over the
place and are pulling up on everything.
Abby is standing for extended periods
on her own. They are so funny and
playful, enjoying each other's company.
They are growing out of everything, and
weigh just a little over seventeen pounds.
Christopher is beginning to grow hair,
Abby is beginning to grow teeth (three
now). They are such precious gifts from
God and they make our hearts melt.
We continue to be ever vigilant and
hopeful and ask for continued prayers.

We ask especially for prayers for the birth mother, as she is trying to complete her first semester away at college with the prospect of having to take two nine-month-old babies back into her life if things don't work out. She has been so selfless in this whole situation, and yet she is the one suffering the most. The power of prayer is very strong and we see it working at every turn. Thank you for your support!

Love,
Valerie, Roger, Abby and Christopher

20

LETTERS TO THE TRIBE

After repeated, unanswered calls to the tribe's attorney to find out the outcome of their meeting to determine whom the tribe would support, I didn't think it would hurt us a bit if we orchestrated a tribal blitz of letters, phone calls and faxes on our behalf, all on the same day.

We also sent out a request via email, and posted on our church bulletin board for anyone who knew about Christopher and Abby, to put in a good word for keeping them where they are, in a good, safe, loving and drug-free home.

The response was overwhelming. We must have had one hundred letters to the tribe. The tribe had to know we were not going away.

Email Update - 12/21/04

Dear Friends, Family and Interested Parties,

Many of you have been on our long journey with Abby and Christopher and have asked if there is anything you can do. While we all feel helpless at times, small things may make a big difference. This may not win the case, but you never know how it may help.

When we asked the Choctaw Nation what they had done to investigate the birth father, they commented that they had received some pictures of the babies with letters from the family. They had also received letters from people who knew the birth father. We felt they had ignored the police reports we sent regarding his drug use, and were supporting the birth father based upon a few letters of recommendation.

The influence of whom the Choctaw Nation decides to support is significant. Our hope is that they will actively support us rather than the birth father, as our home would be the best place for the children; free from drugs, guns and documented domestic violence. We are asking you to send a letter to the tribe, copying the Chief and the person responsible for our case at the tribe. We want the tribe to be inundated with correspondence about this case prior to the next hearing on January 6. You can fax and mail your letters before that time to the following: ...If you happen to be Choctaw, feel free to mention how disappointed you are that your tribe would even consider taking the children out of the secure and loving home where they have lived most of their lives.

Why would they take them from a loving Choctaw home filled with rich tribal history to place them in a home with a family of questionable morals, ethics and a disturbing history of domestic abuse and drug use? Even if you are not Choctaw, you know the facts from the newspaper article, or what we have told you about the father's drug use and his lack of support for the mother during her pregnancy.

We so appreciate your support and your ability to help us fight the good fight to keep these kids where they belong!

Love,
Valerie, Roger, Abby and Christopher

21

AMBUSH TWO

Thirty days had come and gone. I would call every day, and sometimes twice, to talk to Director Miller and the Chief. They were avoiding us like the plague. Our great meeting with the Nathan Miller had left us so much hope. Now it seemed it was all a big mistake and he had the eraser to make it all go away. I had no idea how complicated this was.

The tribe's headquarters in Durant was over three hours away. So we could not just drop by. Or could we? Roger called one final time and said we would be coming to Durant with our lawyer, and we wanted to meet with Mr. Miller again.

We were getting nervous. At this point, we were going to have to subpoena Mr. Miller to testify about what he'd previously told us in his office. Before we appeared in court, we wanted to know where he stood, and whom the tribe was going to support. Roger's call did the trick and the meeting was scheduled.

At our initial meeting, we had met a warm, forthright and friendly man with free-flowing information about what had happened. We don't know what changed, but when we arrived for this second meeting, bringing Noel and Sabra along with us, the Director was still cordial, but now tight-lipped, and in the company of additional representatives from the tribe's Family Services Division. We assumed he had been given some sort of gag order for our meeting as he said very little. We left feeling very uneasy; our euphoria from the first meeting with him was gone.

Both the Director and the Chief were subpoenaed to testify at the December 7th hearing, and we had no idea what they were going to say. We knew if they supported any of the birth father's family, we might never finish fighting with their entire bloodline, which I had learned was the intent of the ICWA placement preference.

Email Update - 12/03/04

Dear Friends and Family,
I am too tired to write much from the meeting today. Not surprisingly, the tribe had changed their tune and had planned answers for what had happened. They say that their attorney was contracted for the tribe through the Family Services department, that he denied any connection with the birth father's family,

and that we must have misunderstood some of the things he said.

All of the pages and pages of information on the birth father's family were minimized and called hearsay. However, my own memory was enhanced with my personal and copious note taking.

The bottom line is that they know whom they are going to support, but they cannot tell us until the hearing next Tuesday. The babies' best interest is their main priority, and secondly the rights of the birth father, only in the sense that they want to make sure his rights were not violated through the process of the Indian Child Welfare Act.

They did say that in court, their attorney would have to clarify that he is there ONLY on behalf of the tribe, the babies, and NOT the birth father. And that the birth father will essentially have to fend for himself on the issue of best interest of the kids (i.e. his ability to parent, drug use, etc.) Our contact will be coming to court next week to testify in our Motion to Disqualify the tribe's lawyer's son. We get a sense that they want out of this and to backtrack what their lawyer has said and done. But they are going to have to keep him now and try to fix the situation from this point forward. We have been warned that this may drag on until well after the kids' first birthday, but we will persevere. Thanks for all of your encouragement. Keep the prayers coming, especially next week on the seventh... More to come.

Love,
Valerie, Roger, Abby and Christopher

22

PEARL HARBOR DAY HEARING
12/01/04

Hearing dates always made us so anxious. If the hearings are continued, as often happens, it gives us a sense of vertigo as we lose some of our momentum. If they do happen, we hold our breath, knowing the outcome could forever alter our lives.

Today, we drove forty-five minutes to the courthouse with sweaty palms, upset stomachs, headaches, and frazzled nerves. We had the habit each time we made the trip, to pray Thy Will Be Done. Silently, because I didn't want to freak out Roger, I prayed for angels to surround the courthouse before the hearing, and to keep all evil from entering.

Later, Roger told me he silently prayed for St. George and his soldiers to surround the courthouse to prevent evil from entering the courthouse, too. I closed my eyes and visualized thousands of white angels with wings spread, touching tip to tip, forming a huge dome, almost like you see when someone's house is covered in a giant bubble to be fumigated. No gaps. No holes for any bad thing to enter.

I prayed for God's presence, along with Mary, and any other Saint of the day. (Father John had been telling us which Saint's Feast Days corresponded with our court dates.) I would look up the Saint's name, and it was always so ironic how their story mirrored what we were going through that day. In reading about them, we knew our challenge and the anxiety we were having had been felt by many before us in even greater ways.

At the courthouse, we tried to drive around a few times to see if we could spot the birth father's family so we wouldn't have to park by them, or walk in with them. We went through the doors and were greeted by uniformed officers ready to pat us down as we emptied our pockets to walk through the metal detectors.

They took my heavy portable file cabinet with manila files categorized by topic: transcripts, motions, case law, files on each person, and sent it down the conveyor belt to be x-rayed. They saw highlighters, sticky notes, paper clips and pens. I was prepared to assist Noel with anything she might have needed. This was our life, our one case, whereas Noel had many other cases.

We rode the elevators to the second floor and the big waiting area, checking to see who was there first. There were scratchy, worn out chairs with old magazines on low, round oak tables, typical of small town, country courthouses. We waited.

One by one, we snuck down to the courtroom and

peeked through the small rectangular windows on the doors to see if anyone else was there. We were finally motioned in. We walked halfway down the middle aisle of the courtroom and pushed open the wooden, knee-high swinging doors.

Noel was on my right, and Roger my left. There were two conference tables along the side of the courtroom. We sat at the big conference table behind the birth father and his attorney. I was glad they were not behind us, staring at the back of our necks.

The courtroom was like a small church, with several rows of pews split by one center aisle. Nicole and her parents, along with Sabra, always sat directly behind the partition in lockstep support of us. We would turn around and whisper to Nicole before the judge would come in.

The birth father and his family would whisper together, also. It was horrible. If I had been in Nicole's shoes, I don't think I could have done it. She was only nineteen, and here she was in a courtroom with the boy who had put her through so much, just steps away.

The birth father did not really want to raise Christopher and Abby. He had stated he would give them to his mom to raise. We already knew the example she had provided for her other kids. Now, she wanted to take a shot at our two little ones. Roger and I weren't about to sit by and let that happen.

The birth father's family also requested from the judge, unsupervised visitation over the holidays. That fist in my stomach gripped tighter at the thought of

Christopher and Abby being away from us, especially in such an environment. *Unsupervised?*

Thankfully, the judge did not allow it. Victory! *Maybe this judge was going to be okay after all.*

Email Update - 12/07/04

Dear Friends and Family,
Thank you for your prayers today, as
they are working. Small victories keep
us going.

Today our Choctaw Nation contact
who was subpoenaed to testify did not
show up due to a funeral he had to
attend. Fortunately, for us, none of the
hearings could take place today, as the
hearing to discuss the tribe's lawyer
had to have this key witness.

The judge couldn't do anything
without knowing what the tribe's
position was. It has been rescheduled
for January 6, and if this date falls
through, it will be February 22. The
lawyer did state he represented
the tribe, and the tribe's interests
were aligned with the birth father.
The other piece of good news is that
although visitation was not stopped, the
judge made it clear that only the birth
father and his parents are able to come
to visitation. No more aunts, uncles,
cousins, girlfriends, great grandparents,
other grandchildren, etc. Since we had a
messed up schedule this week, we offered
them four hours on Friday (instead of

the usual two two-hour visits) and they declined. They said they just wanted two hours.

As usual, the birth father's family repeatedly tried to intimidate Nicole and her family when the court reporter, the judge and the lawyers all left the room by loudly saying, "They will learn not to mess with us; we'll show them. They'd better be careful." Anyway, we still have many different options, and this was good news today. We are looking forward to a relatively quiet holiday to enjoy the reason for the season.

Happy holidays to all!

Love,
Valerie, Roger, Abby and Christopher

23

ROGER-DAR

Roger has a way about him. He is intuitive. I am not. I wear rose-colored glasses and think everyone I meet is great until they prove otherwise. He doesn't give much thought to people he meets until they prove to be trustworthy.

My friends will ask if they can just drop by with their new boyfriends to return a 'borrowed book' or some other made-up story in hopes Roger will answer the door and turn on his Roger radar (or Roger-dar) for just a minute.

Up to this point, I thought he was cynical, picky, and didn't like very many people. Now I know he's just very intuitive. But it has taken me years and many times of being wrong about people to recognize his gift.

We disagreed about our judge. I thought he was a nice man who would be fair. After all, he was a prominent, well-known adoption judge. He was not going to be easy on biological fathers with so little regard for birth mothers and their children that they continue to take drugs and spend money that could be better spent on supporting children.

Or was he? Roger was skeptical from the beginning, and said at the time he felt our judge would not be a friend to us. *How did he know that? He wasn't even giving him a chance.* I don't know when I started to listen to Roger's intuition. Maybe when things he predicted years ago started happening. I hoped he would be wrong about our judge. But he wasn't.

24

MORE VISITATIONS

I don't remember how many visitations we had to endure, and I didn't journal much about them because they were probably the most painful and stressful part of our ordeal. We suffered through getting the kids dressed, packing diaper bag with toys and bottles for the birth father and his mom to use, and butterflies in my stomach.

For our visits, we used the back entrance to Catholic Charities so we didn't have to run into the birth father. Each time, we passed off the baby carriers to Sabra, who then took them to the conference room for the next two hours.

We would sit in Sabra's office, waiting, hearing cries from Christopher and Abby of discomfort, hunger, and fear. We could not go comfort them. No one could comfort us.

Strange things happened at the visits, according to Sabra. Although Sabra supervised the family at Catholic Charities, they would take the children's clothes off in the cold conference room and put them in other clothes, take their pictures, and change them back again.

Instead of letting them play with their toys that we sent, they brought loud, bright, flashing toys, inappropriate for their age, and held them in their faces to get them to stop crying.

During one visit, the birth father passed out and slept the entire time. On another visit, the family brought Kool-aid in a bottle, along with chocolate chip cookies. Christopher and Abby were six months old at the time, and had no teeth! Many times, the family also tried to bring more than the allowed two visitors.

Christopher usually passed out and slept through the visits; his way of dealing with stress. But each visit ended with both kids crying. By the time we got them back in the car to go home, they were comatose.

One visit was especially rough. The birth father was very belligerent and not following the visitation ground rules. The visitation room was one large room on the third floor with tables, chairs, a television and toys. The ground rules were that neither he nor his mother could leave the room with the children. (We were always wary that he would try to walk or run out with the kids.)

That day, he had one baby under each arm and was walking around, headed for the door. Luckily, Sabra came back in to the room after being out for a minute, and tried to keep him from leaving. He said in an argumentative tone, "I can walk any where I want."

Sabra advised him to get back in the room but he ignored her. Sabra suspected he might be on some sort of drugs and was concerned for the babies' safety as well as her own. She called the Executive Director of the agency to intervene. He did, and the visit was over.

We requested that the birth father submit to a drug test, which the court ordered, and his family argued against it, due to cost. We offered to pay, and the court ordered the hair follicle test. We expected to find marijuana in his system.

These visits continued to take a toll on the babies and us. They made no noises on the return home, would not nap, and took several days to get back on their scheduled naps and mealtimes. Christopher rocked himself back and forth, and would stare straight ahead. Neither were sleeping through the night anymore.

Just when it seemed things would calm down, it was time for another round of visits. What was anyone getting out of this? It did not appear to us that any bonding was going on.

*　*　*

Roger called me on my cell phone while I was at work and said, "Go stand by your fax machine".

Okay, I thought, what's up? I stood staring at the paper as it slowly inched out Quest Diagnostics Drug Test Results. I didn't realize we were getting results for the birth father's court-ordered drug tests today. I scanned the list of substances for marijuana in the birth father's urine. Zero. My heart fell. Roger, still on the phone, told me to look at the top—Methamphetamine.

What was that?

Whatever it was, the birth father's level was off the charts. The minimum threshold to register as a drug in someone's system is 300 picograms. Birth father's result was over 8,900, which indicated regular use.

This explained his erratic behavior during the visitations, over stimulating the kids with noisy and flashing toys, and sleeping during the visits in the middle of the day. Later, we found out this hostile and unpredictable attitude was called 'tweaking.'

We thought back to the first time we saw him in person, and how over time he had changed from a healthy looking young man to just a hanger for an ill-fitting suit with an ashen face, covered with open sores.

Journal - 12/23/04

Because the family declined the four-hour visitation we offered last time, we went for the scheduled two-hour visitation today. The birth father and his mom decided they wanted to see, if the babies were not fussy, if they could extend the visit. We agreed, but said it must be either two or four hours, as I had not prepared for four hours, and would need to go home to get the food and diapers. They called their lawyer to complain that they were forced to spend four hours visiting the kids. Forced to visit??

Journal – 12/30/04

We do not know much about Meth, so we are researching the drug and it scares the hell out of us. We are concerned for the safety of the kids, as well as for us. The birth father's attorney called the place that did the drug testing and told them that the birth father had taken Ambien, and asked if it could cause it to be positive? They said that Ambien is a barbiturate, and Meth is an amphetamine.

He must have taken the Ambien to help him sleep since Meth can cause you to stay awake for days on end.

2005

POTHOLES IN THE ROAD

25

EPIPHANY!

Email Update – 01/06/05

Dear All,

Well, it is fitting that the last hearing was on Pearl Harbor Day and that today's hearing was on Epiphany, the day of the baptism of Christ. I prayed that the judge and the tribe would have an Epiphany of their own, and they did. Thanks to your prayers and letters, we claim victory!

The first item of business on the court docket was to disqualify the tribe's lawyer. The tribe's representatives and their lawyer flew up from Durant, ready to make a deal. In lieu of getting into messy testimony and asking us to drop our motion, the tribe chose to take a neutral position. They told the court that they did not support one tribal member over the other, and that they would let the judge make his determination without their involvement, as long as the ICWA was followed.

If the judge determined that there was good reason not to place Abby and Christopher with the birth father, the tribe would not intervene.

They said they supported continued placement of the babies in our home for the duration of the proceedings, regardless of how long they take. They have done a 180-degree turn from the beginning when they had requested that the babies be removed from our home and placed with the birth father or his family.

Their jaws dropped when the tribe's lawyer told the birth father's family they could no longer support any of them. The tribe breezed out as fast as they could to fly back to Durant.

Item number two was the Motion to Stay, which we won. This motion was to stop the Custody Hearing while the Appeal was heard. If we win the Appeal, it means that the birth father's consent is not necessary for adoption and we can proceed to terminate his parental rights. However, while the birth father would be out of the picture, we would then start over, fighting his parents for custody to follow the ICWA. Again, a major victory, as the Appeal could take three to five months for a decision to be made. If we lose the Appeal, we still have several options.

In the meantime, there was no Custody Hearing, no expert witnesses, and not much discussion of the drug test results we were prepared to use. However, the birth father was prepared to dispute the results of the positive Meth results, as evidenced by the bottles and boxes of every cold medicine available on the table before him.

His lawyer was going to argue how cold medicines produce false positives in hair follicle tests.

Unfortunately, visitation was not stopped. Fortunately, though, it will be at a new location with supervision, for which the birth father will pay each week. He will be subjected to two weekly scheduled urine drug tests and one random test, as well as one hair follicle test per month, which he also must pay. They had requested many additional people to visit, which was not granted. Another victory! As you can see, it is not over, and we may expect it to go on another year. However, each day is another day with Abby and Christopher. We will be able to experience their first birthday and their first steps. We are overjoyed and excited about the prospect of being able to sleep at night for several months to come. Never give up, never give in! May God Bless each of you on this blessed day!

Love,
Valerie, Roger, Abby and Christopher

26

THE BOULDER IN THE ROAD

"Why?" everyone asked, "would the tribe, after they were made acutely aware of the birth father's drug use and other questionable family issues, continue to support him?"

It was only at the last moment, when we forced the issue that the tribe withdrew their support of the birth father and stated to the District Court that their position had changed from 'supporting the birth father' to being 'neutral'; they would accept placement in either home.

Equal playing field? Just because the birth father and Roger were both members of the Choctaw tribe? Now, being considered 'as good as' the birth father was unnerving, considering the fact that our home was free from drug use and violence, and the only place the children felt safe and secure.

It begs the question of what the birth father would have to do for the tribe NOT to consider him an acceptable parent and choose to throw support our way. At what point were the children's needs considered first and ICWA second?

This is a troubling question with a more troubling answer. The tribe's obligation, according to ICWA, is Placement Preference. They must follow the Act in the case their tribe member brings to them. It does not matter what the biological parents wish, even if they are both Native American and want to place their child someplace different than the tribe does.

Noel couldn't remember a case where the tribe changed sides to support a non-biological relative or non-tribe selected home. Her perspective is that it is a victory for us for them to be neutral and wash their hands of the case, waiving their Placement Preference. I guess when you see cases like this on a regular basis, you learn to claim victory within the parameters you are given.

We are concerned that there are so many other people in similar situations that do not have the resolve or resources to fight like we do. We cringe every time we hear a story where children are caught in the middle of this law and are ripped from one known family entity to be placed with an unknown, and on occasion, in a harmful situation.

What is ICWA? Laws take on a life of their own when courts interpret them without considering Congress' original intent. In my opinion, it was never the intent of Congress to tear families apart, especially when a family member has as little as 1-2 percent Native American blood, and may have never resided in a Native American home or on a reservation. I never in my wildest dreams thought I would have to consider how a federal law would impact the fate of my family.

27

THE BAPTISM

In our church, babies are usually baptized when they are around six months old. (Nicole, sharing similar religious beliefs, had graciously given us permission for baptism.) However, with us in limbo and not having custody, guardianship, or any real parental status, getting permission from our Church was a little more complicated. Father John took our request up the church ladder, requesting special permission. Finally, our request was approved and we were able to baptize Abby and Christopher around their first birthday. It was a joyous occasion.

Email Update - 03/14/05

Dear Friends and Family,
I know it has been a while since I sent
an update, so I have good and hopeful

news. Hopefully this won't reach you too late to be able to keep us in your morning prayers. The hopeful news... We have a court hearing in the morning regarding visitation. At the last hearing on January 6th, visitation parameters were established for supervision in a location at which both parties agreed, weekly drug testing, etc. It seems like we can't agree on a location. The one we initially selected was $50 an hour for a qualified Licensed Counselor Social Worker (LCSW) near the house and convenient for the babies.

They countered with a place thirty minutes away for $20 an hour that was supervised, but the counselor's stance on drug use being 'whatever you do before you get here and after you leave is your own business,' was not acceptable to us. Our counter offer was a place convenient for the babies, that had a strict, no drug use policy.

They also have a new lawyer in the picture. Apparently, they still have their original lawyer, but the birth father's mom wanted her own lawyer, too. We'll find out how that works in the morning. The new twist we hear coming up tomorrow is that the birth father has enrolled in Vo-Tech from 9 a.m. -3 p.m. every day of the week, claiming the classes are available only during the day. I'm sure they are shooting for unsupervised visitation on the weekends, our precious time with them when they are awake.

Has anyone ever read about Meth and the after effects of using? (The birth father's most recent hair test was negative after the last two being positive. But only after he cut his hair extremely short.) We discovered that if a user is 'off' for a time, it is not pretty. Addicts hit a 'wall' up to 120 days after using and they can be deeply depressed, suicidal, and possibly violent. Not what we want for Abby and Christopher.

So the hopeful news is that the judge will do what is right and best for the kids, and that God's will be done.

Prayers are needed again for the strength of the birth mother and her parents who are constantly challenged with the decision to leave the babies with us. We are still a couple of months away from getting a decision from the Court of Appeals. The good news... Abby and Christopher turned one, and are officially Greek

Orthodox Christians! It was a beautiful baptism ceremony, and there is a picture of Abby in a dress her Nouna (Godmother) and her Nouna's mother made out of my wedding dress and veil. It has such special meaning to me.

Abby was a little angel, as was Christopher, but he just didn't smile for the camera as much; he wasn't happy about wearing his baptism hat! We thought they were perfect and the occasion will be cherished forever.

They are walking all over the place, eating more solids, popping out teeth right and left (six each), and babbling up a storm to each other. In spite of the stress and strain, we are so blessed to feel their hugs, loving glances, and their demanding pleas for more Cheerios. We really couldn't ask for more, as we know how blessed we are.

Love,
Valerie, Roger, Abby and Christopher

28

PRAYERS HEARD

Email Update - 03/15/05

Dear Friends and Family,
Thank you, thank you, thank you!!
For those of you that sent prayers and
thoughts our way this morning for court
– they worked!! After two hours back
and forth in the judge's chambers, we got
what we wanted on visitation: visitation
supervised at the location closest to our
home.

The issue of the birth father enrolling
in Vo-Tech never entered into the picture.
The other story I have to share is one the
birth mother shared with us today, as we
often share 'God winks.'

The birth mother was walking to

class last Thursday and she was in a hurry. So she cut through a parking lot. It was a windy day. As she was walking, she noticed a picture of Jesus on the ground on a prayer card. She did not pick it up, and kept walking quickly to class, forgetting about it. The next day, on the same walk, the same shortcut, and the same wind, she found the same picture of Jesus.

How it didn't blow away, she didn't know. This time she did pick it up. It had been stepped on and was rough from the bumpy concrete pressing through. She turned it over and on the back was a quote telling her that Jesus was there for her to see her through difficult times with family. You might remember last Friday was the day of the babies' birth, one year ago.

Love,
Valerie, Roger, Abby and Christopher

Journal - 3/25/05

Abby audibly said 'baby.' She didn't really know what she was saying, but it was clear!

29

NEW INFO

Email Update - 05/10/05

Dear Friends and Family,
Abby and Christopher are doing great.
They are running around and getting
into everything, especially the cabinet
with all of their snacks. They bring us
containers of Goldfish, Cheerios and
even dog treats hoping we will open
them and give them a snack. (Don't
worry; we don't let them eat the dog
treats.)

We are still impatiently awaiting
the decision on the Appeal. Tomorrow
marks a major milestone for us. It
is Christopher and Abby's fourteen-
month birthday. The reason it is so

important is that there is a different statute that will allow a non-custodial parent's rights to be terminated if they have not had substantial compliance contributing to the support of their biological children for twelve out of fourteen months prior to a petition for adoption being filed. Not one dime has been paid to date.

So, if the Appeal comes back against us saying that the birth father's consent is necessary for the adoption, we have this card to play. Even with the birth father's rights terminated, we will still have to fight for custody against his parents because of the Indian Child Welfare Act. We are ready to do this!

Even though the birth father and his mother continue to show up weekly for supervised visitation, the birth father continues to live with his parents and he continues to test positive for Meth. His parents are not getting him any help or drug rehab, and are willing to take on two more kids?

Birth mother is doing great in school and patiently seeing this through with us. Keep her in your prayers. We are having so much fun cherishing our family and my new job allows me so much more time with the kids...making life even better.

Love,
Valerie, Roger, Abby and Christopher

30

OUR LOSS IN THE APPELLATE COURT

Email Update - 05/24/05

Dear Friends and Family,
We lost the Appeal! *We learned today that two out of three judges in the Court of Appeals believe that $139 worth of gifts given to a birth mother during a pregnancy constitutes 'support.' But it's not over. We are moving to Plan B, (or C, or D...), and will continue to fight. Our Appeal had been to determine if the birth father's consent was necessary for the adoption, based upon any support he contributed during the birth mother's pregnancy. He has not supported the children with any money for the past fourteen months, which should give us enough ammo to terminate his rights*

and file another case under a different statute. If that doesn't work, we hope the numerous positive Meth tests will seal the deal. Then we will take on his parents in our fight for custody. We are having so much fun and enjoying every minute we have together with the kids. Please keep the birth mother in your prayers, especially as she cannot comprehend a law that favors people who provide no financial support whatsoever for their offspring. We appreciate your continued support and prayers.

Love,
Valerie, Roger, Abby and Christopher

Journal - 06/25/05

We went to the zoo today for the first time. Christopher loved the King Vultures and the funny orange blobs hanging off their noses. Abby loved the monkeys and watched them intently.

Journal - 06/27/05

For the last several months, we have gotten into a routine taking Christopher and Abby to visitation with the birth father and his mom at the new location. Gray and Craig have been our Monday morning greeters, and try to assure us that after we leave, Christopher and Abby stop crying and calm down and play.

I can only remember all of the times that I heard their non-stop cries as I ran to the bathroom with an upset stomach, counting the minutes until the agony was over.

The visits are supervised, with the counselor behind a one-way mirror so he can see and hear everything going on. The counselor says the family still continues their overstimulation. But the strange thing is they bring their noisy toys, change the children clothes into the clothes they bring, and tell Christopher and Abby that they bought them those things and they are theirs to keep. But they will never send anything home with them.

Our lawyer holds us back from filing a plethora of motions against the birth father for non-compliance: failure to produce the requested financials (court-ordered in December), not supporting Christopher and Abby for x *producing results from urine and hair drug tests for over two months. We are so frustrated with the fact that the birth father and his family continually defy the court orders with no penalty.*

31

VISITATION HEARINGS, HEADACHES & HEARTACHES

Email Update - 08/11/05

Dear Friends and Family,
Things have been fairly quiet for the last few months with regards to our legal action and the twins. We have enjoyed a summer break from visitation since the visitation facility lost their intern, and the price jumped from $20 an hour to $80 an hour.

The birth father and his mom said they couldn't afford to pay, so they chose not to see the kids each week, even for an hour. We had asked the Court of Appeals to reconsider their decision to uphold the District Court's decision that the birth father's consent was necessary for the adoption due to his support during the pregnancy. We lost the Appeal and rehearing. So now, we are waiting to hear from the State Supreme Court when they return from recess in September.

We went to court last Monday, August 1, to discuss the birth father's Motion to Expand Visitation to be unsupervised all day at their home. The family had also filed other things that were procedurally incorrect as the State Supreme Court has not made their final decision. With another hearing on August 24 for a Motion to Suspend Visitation (due to the continued Meth use), the judge has decided to hear everything on that day.

It was so nerve-wracking and felt very threatening to sit in the same courtroom with the birth father and his family across the aisle, once again making sure we could hear the birth father's threat to 'get them babies.'

In the meantime, we were told by our lawyer to expect to continue visitation until it is all resolved, and that we need to consider another visitation supervisor which the judge and the babies' lawyer recommended who is well respected and only $10 per hour.

We agreed to visit with her. Before we could even get her name and number, she had contacted us and told us she was court ordered to supervise visitation on Saturday. She stated that she was involved in this case 'because the kids are going to be returned to their birth father.'

You can only imagine our surprise, anger, and frustration. After much agony and investigating, we found out that the birth father's mother had called this supervisor and given her erroneous information regarding the case. Needless to say, they did not get visitation, and will wait until things are done properly. This peaked our frustration. Instead of waiting for the State Supreme Court to make their decision when they returned from break, we went ahead and filed OUR Petition to Adopt the children. Catholic Charities was unsuccessful in terminating the birth father's rights in court. We considered this our first loss, even though we were not a named party in the case.

The birth mother filed a Motion for Arrearages for the birth father to pay back child support and reimburse expenses, which now add up to $20,000. We also filed a Petition to Terminate the *birth father's parental rights as he has not paid any support since the babies were born. We don't know when this court date will be, but we ask for extra prayers, as we get closer to the heart of the matter.*

Christopher is now making the sign of the cross before we say the Lord's Prayer at night, and is kissing his Guardian Angel Icon before bed. Abby continues to do the opposite of what we tell her to do, smiling and goo-goo gooing all the way. They say a few random words here and there and are just so much fun. I am just so grateful that they will not remember the stress and strain of this battle. Hopefully, this struggle will be over before they go to school!

Love,
Valerie, Roger, Abby and Christopher

Email Update- 10/11/05

Hello Friends and Family,
We had another day in court today. Our head is spinning from all of the items discussed, and those put off. We had many things on the agenda today, mainly about visitation. It appears the family could not afford two attorneys,

so only their original attorney is now representing the birth father.

We had requested that all pending issues be 'stayed,' pending the outcome of our first case, which is now with the State Supreme Court of Oklahoma. We were waiting for them to either agree with the District and Appellate Courts, which had both ruled that the birth father's consent was necessary for the adoption to proceed based upon the fact that he gave $139 in gifts during the birth mother's pregnancy.

It is so sad that a precedent has been set that allows an unemployed, drug-addicted birth father to contribute little more than $10 a month, while retaining the right to force the birth mother to parent her children.

While some issues can be frozen until then, the judge denied our request to stay the issues regarding visitation. The birth father requested that visitation be expanded to be able to take the kids to their home on a weekend day. This was denied. A victory for us!

We requested that visitation be stopped due to drug use. Unfortunately, we lost on this one for several reasons, primarily because the birth father has had a few months of negative drug results, and we weren't able to present anything on this issue.

His family had also filed a Contempt Citation against us, saying we had refused visitation the past several months. This is unfounded and untrue. The Contempt trial is set for January.

In the meantime, we have to resume visitationinafewweeks,withstipulations that the birth father pass three urine tests this week, three next week and a hair follicle drug test too. Based on his behavior today, he seems to be back on. We requested the court to order the birth father's permission for us to get passports for the kids. We are planning a vacation to the Caribbean in December.

The babies' lawyer (Guardian Ad Litem) agreed that there was no harm in this, as did the judge, who ruled in our favor, with stipulations that we put up a $10,000 surety bond to make sure we come back! The birth father was very upset and refused to sign. At that time, his lawyer said he would go to jail if he did not.

He stated he didn't care and he wasn't signing. He eventually was persuaded by his mom, and scribbled on the pages while threatening loudly that he would sign it, but he was going to make sure we never went. I feel certain that his angry scrawl of a signature is now permanently etched into the surface of the oak courtroom table. He then stormed out of the courtroom.

Our next hearing is on October 31st. Trick or Treat! We will be putting forth our Motion to Compel (trying to make the judge make the birth father give us the information we requested for the next trial). We are still waiting on things from last December, so I don't know if it will do much good. The next hearing of substance is on November 21, which is the Presentation of the Virgin Mary in our church. This is the 'Big One' hearing and we need you to pull out all the stops for prayers. We are trying to get the birth father's parental rights terminated based upon the fact that he has not paid any support since the babies' birth nineteen months ago.

If we actually win the State Supreme Court case, this won't be needed. But we may not hear anything about that until after this case. We feel we have a pretty good chance, but we thought we had good chances today on a few issues, and we lost. So there are no guarantees.

Birth mother is doing great. She is keeping her grades high and continues to be very supportive while going through a lot. I really don't know how she does it. So, please keep her in your prayers, too.

Love,
Valerie, Roger, Abby and Christopher

32

AN UP DAY ON THE COURTROOM ROLLER COASTER RIDE

You know by now how I like to put everything in an Excel spreadsheet. *I have my good friend Mickey to thank for this obsession, but it does help me visualize patterns.* I had to create a spreadsheet on the birth father's urine and hair follicle drug testing, including dates, types and results, and highlighting all of the positive tests, or missed tests.

It became quite a handy document and did show a clear pattern of continued use and abuse that could not be explained by poppy seeds, cold medicine, sleeping pills or other excuses for the truth. As I once learned, "Facts don't cease to exist because they are ignored." In other words, 'denial.'

Email Update - 10/18/05

Dear Friends and Family,
A brief update to the news below...We called the lab to find out why the birth father didn't have a September hair follicle test, (my spreadsheet showed a blank space for September results) and they said he did take one, and it was positive for Meth! It looks like he withheld that piece of information on our day in court. The information would have made the outcome very different. We will present this info on October 31.

Love,
Valerie, Roger, Abby and Christopher

Journal - 10/31/05

The hearing could not have gone any better – Victory #1.– The family had filed a Contempt Citation against us for not complying with visitation, and the penalty was a $2,500 bond. We have, of course, followed the court orders to the letter. It is up to them to prove to the contrary.
The judge changed the bond to OR (Own Recognizance) and we don't have

to pay anything. (I never thought I would ever be in a courtroom where my name and 'Own Recognizance' were used in the same sentence. Surreal.)

Victory #2. – Motion to Compel – The birth father was ordered to provide information regarding his interrogatory by November 7 at 5 p.m., or he can't use the information to defend himself in the November 21 hearing.

Victory #3 – Motion to Disqualify – They wanted this case dropped, citing it had already been lost in State Supreme Court, or res judicata. However, we were successful in arguing that this is a new case with new statutes. The judge agreed.

Victory #4 – Motion to Suspend Visitation – The birth father agreed that we shouldn't have to comply with court-ordered visitation since he himself had not complied with court-ordered drug testing. He also said he had never done Meth, and that people on Meth cannot have good judgment to protect their kids. He also said people on Meth should not get to visit their kids, and lied about the drug testing. When asked what the most important thing he had learned in his parenting classes he was taking, he said, "If the kids are crying, you take them to someone else's home." With those statements; no more visitations.

We think this was the first time his grandparents, who were in court, had heard of his drug use and they were very disappointed. His father told him he had made a fool out of himself by lying on the stand about his drug use, and that he was an embarrassment to his family.

33

IF IT SOUNDS
TOO GOOD TO BE TRUE...

Email Update - 11/15/05

Dear Friends and Family,
We are cautiously optimistic and not yet jumping for joy, but we think we have reached an out-of-court agreement with the birth father. After things went so poorly for him in court, he told his lawyer he would consent to the adoption if we gave him visitation one weekend a month and paid some of his lawyer's fees. We did not agree to this because in our hearts we knew it would not be in the children's best interest to have any future contact with the birth father. Besides, we knew that the law stated that any parent consenting to having their parental

rights terminated, could not request or demand any conditions be met before they signed termination papers. We countered their offer with no visitation, no lawyer's fees, period. Several days went by, and finally his lawyer called and said that he agreed to our terms. However, this is not a done deal. We still go to court on November 21, and hope the birth father will voluntarily consent to terminate his parental rights in front of the judge. If he does this, we will go back in front of the judge on December 12 for the final decree. If he changes his mind, which he can still do, we will continue with our hearing to terminate his rights involuntarily. Please continue to pray, as these are the most important dates yet. We are so hopeful that this will be over by Christmas!

Love,
Valerie, Roger, Abby and Christopher

Email Update - 11/21/05

Dear Friends and Family,
Yes, the promise of the birth father

consenting to the adoption was too good to be true. He changed his mind due to the intervention of his mother.

When we got to court today, he fired his lawyer, declared himself indigent, got a court-appointed lawyer and had the hearing postponed until January 20. We will now move forward to Terminate his Parental Rights based upon non-payment of support since the birth of the twins. Holidays will still be happier without required visitation. The continuation of this court date is December 13th.

Love,
Valerie, Roger, Abby and Christopher

34

ONE MORE DAY WITH CHRISTOPHER AND ABBY

Email Update - 12/15/05

Dear Friends and Family,
Well, many of you are wondering what happened at our December 13th hearing, and the answer is nothing! It was continued until January 9th because the birth father's lawyer was not prepared. Of course, we were happy to have it moved out past the holidays.

Abby and Christopher are now twenty-one months old and so much fun to be around. They constantly make us laugh. Christopher' little feet are so smelly – he demands to keep Abby's fuzzy purple butterfly house shoes on when he goes to bed at night. When he wakes up in the morning, they are still on! He also likes to wear Abby's hats.

Abby loves her stickers and won't take them off of her arms and face. I hope these are not signs of things to come....a cross dresser and a tattooed lady!

We have appreciated your continued prayers throughout the year, and wish you and your family a very Merry Christmas!

Love,
Valerie, Roger, Abby and Christopher

LOST

35

DOWN, BUT NOT OUT

Email Update - 01/19/06

Dear Friends and Family,
Things were moving along in court today until we got to the part where the birth father's signature was missing on a very important interrogatory document.

The birth father refused to testify to any income information, so we will need to subpoena his first lawyer and a past and current employer, in addition to getting certified copies of payments from worker's compensation court.

Interestingly enough, the birth father did say he was working, which may change his status of being eligible for free legal representation. (It is perjury to lie on a form saying you are indigent.)

This year on the Orthodox Church calendar, Good Friday is on April 21st, our next court date. I take this as a good sign.

Love,
Valerie, Roger, Abby and Christopher

P.S. In the photos, Christopher loves to wear Abby's hats and Abby has been making Dagwood sandwiches out of cheese, crackers and cookies. The taller the better!!

36

OUT, BUT NOT FOR THE COUNT

Email Update - 04/20/06

Hello Friends and Family,
It has been a while since our last hearing, and we wanted to update you on what is about to happen. We have our hearing in the morning to determine if the birth father's consent is necessary for the adoption. We are focusing solely on whether or not the birth father paid according to his ability during a fourteen-month period after the babies were born.

We feel he did not. If we win and the Court determines his consent is not necessary, we still would have another hearing on the best interest of the children. If we lose, we can appeal the decision because we have undeniable proof of his ability to pay, based upon income records and lack of compliance.

Our Eastern Orthodox Easter is celebrated according to the Julian calendar, and is this Sunday. The significance of Good Friday tomorrow is ever present in our minds and is especially important. We ask for your prayers for God's will, and the best situation for Abby and Christopher. The kids couldn't be better. Abby and Christopher are such fun little people to watch. Abby insists on smelling the flowers on my clothing and jewelry; touching every surface and proclaiming how 'soft' it is. Her vocabulary is growing and she is a little chatterbox.

Christopher cannot eat a meal or go far without his 'pieces' set up just right around his plate. He loves his puzzle pieces of backhoes, tractors, and dump trucks! He also has some Michael Jackson thing going on—wants to wear one glove or an oven mitt around the house. And they love playing outside in the dirt. We will let you know what happens after our hearing.

Love,
Valerie, Roger, Abby and Christopher

Email Update – 04/21/06

Dear Friends and Family,
We lost. *We believe in miracles and that is what we need now! Much to our chagrin and surprise, the judge has ruled that the birth father's consent is necessary for Abby and Christopher to be adopted by us. Of course, the birth father is not inclined to consent.*

The judge made his ruling based upon the fact that during the timeframe in question (fourteen months prior to filing the petition to adopt), the birth father provided financial support to the kids by paying for visitation and court ordered drug testing. His rationale is beyond belief, as these two things do not directly benefit, nor support the children.

If we fail in this direction on an Appeal, we will go in yet another direction. In the two years and nine months this has been going on, not once has anyone discussed the best interests of the children. They are now at an age that disrupting their tiny lives would be very harmful to their growing psyches. (Not to mention ours too!)

Therefore, we are not defeated. We feel fuel has been added to the fire to propel us to further action. Laws need to be changed, and if you have any legislative connections, please let us know.

The kids are doing great. Abby is challenging us lately by incessantly climbing out of her crib. (I know most kids don't stay IN their cribs this long.) We are putting together some 'big kid beds' and for now, they are using the mattresses as slides and Evil Knievel ramps for their toy horses and motorcycles.

Abby crawled out of her crib during naptime one day and got her hands on the Boudreau's Butt Paste diaper rash cream. She thought it was lip-gloss and face cream. It burned a little and was in her hair and all over her pants. This was our signal to remove all items not used for sleeping from their room.

Abby also crawls into Christopher's crib and steals his toys! Christopher has not yet ventured out of his crib. Maybe because he can't move with Abby standing on him in his crib. We will be enrolling him in self-defense classes as soon as we are able!

For some reason, Christopher can say Papa really well, but has a hard time

with 'Muzzie' (Grandma's nickname).
We asked him who Grandma was, and
he said 'Boss.'

He also slurs together BossaPapa.
Who knows where he got that, but Papa
says she IS the boss of him. Christopher
is such a kind, little old soul who loves
to go to church and constantly kiss the
icons and makes the sign of the cross.
In addition to asking you for prayers,
we ask for the special intercession
of Mary, (my inspiration) especially
in this season of Christ's crucifixion.
We wish you all a very Happy Easter,
for we are blessed to have you in our
lives.

Love,
Valerie, Roger, Abby and Christopher

After this long, hard fight, we were then stunned
that our judge made a ruling in the birth father's favor.
This was a huge setback. How could we have come
this far, only to be faced with this incomprehensible
decision? The Court required that all of the birth father's
contact with the twins be supervised by a third party
due to his continued drug usage. He was also ordered to
pay expenses for the supervision and drug testing. How
could the judge say that paying a pittance for supervision
is benefiting Christopher and Abby?

We were shocked beyond belief. *Thy Will Be Done, Never Give Up, Never Give In, It's a Marathon, not a Sprint.* I kept repeating all of these things, but we were tired! I felt like we were wandering down an unpaved road without a map. I had no idea where to go.

No two cases are alike. People asked us constantly how we get through this. You just do it. We don't even think of the other alternative. I used to plan years down the line, but that line has gotten shorter and shorter. If I can get through the next hour, I will think about the next one...and so on.

In addition, I have picked up some bad habits, mainly frequent Starbucks visits. And, with all of our visits to the mall, we have to go to the Godiva store. I bought a pad of sticky notes that say, "If I could combine coffee, chocolate and wine, I would only have one vice." So true!

37

CHRISTOPHER BEFORE

At around age three when Christopher started Mother's Day Out, we began to notice changes in his behavior. Our pediatrician noticed changes as well, and referred us to an early intervention program called Sooner Start that evalutated emotional and developmental milestones. There was concern of a sensory disorder. Sooner Start started coming for regular visits over several months to work with Christopher.

However, after several weeks of counseling and therapy, testing and evaluation, we determined Christopher had *situational, trauma-based anxiety,* brought on by the past visitations where there had been a significant amount of overstimulation and anxiety of strangers.

On a normal day, Christopher behaved like a typical toddler for his age and was developmentally on track. In a situation where non-family or total strangers are encountered, he changed dramatically and became totally withdrawn, non-responsive, non-verbal, lying on the floor in the fetal position, spitting or slobbering with his hand almost completely in his mouth, crying and difficult to console at the extreme.

In situations that made him anxious, especially when there were non-family members present, he buried his head in our chests, demanded to be held, and swayed his strong little body in the direction he wanted to be carried, all while grunting loudly. His anxiety was reduced only through repetitive rocking and swaying, or removing him totally from the situation.

Journal - 03/28/06 – 04/01/06

Sabra came this week to update our home study. Christopher had a very negative reaction to her and would not enter the room, regressing to grunting and moaning, moving his body to get in another room as one of us held him. Since his hospital stay for pneumonia a few of weeks ago, he has had additional setbacks with anxiety and strangers.

He had just started to warm up a little with Ellen from Sooner Start. We try to go to the mall as often as possible to at least get him around and used to strangers. We have been told that a normal life as we know it (but ours is really not 'normal') is over.

We will not be able to travel, to go out to eat, or to subject Christopher to situations where he will be triggered to react defensively like he does. It makes me sick that the visitations have caused this precious little boy to suffer for the rest of his life.

38

THE MIRACLE-
CHRISTOPHER AFTER

As we carried on our day-to-day lives adjusting to our new normal, we read books, researched schools, continued therapy and invested in mini trampolines for Christopher to jump on to reduce his anxiety before heading to a place where there would be strangers. I was amazed at how many things were considered sensory issues. The color of food—Christopher would only eat white things, the textures, sights, smells, the touch—he wanted to run into the Christmas tree to feel the sensation of the sharp needles. He did not like loud noises or flashing lights. We just got used to these things.

It was the day that Christopher jumped from the fireplace hearth into the arms of our handyman, Lee, that we knew a miracle had happened. Lee was a stranger. Even though he had been to the house many times, Christopher never warmed up to him. But why was this time different?

Abby was having fun jumping to Lee and Christopher inched over to see what all the fun was about. He wasn't usually lured into fun, even if Abby was having it. But up he went, and just jumped for Lee to catch him. I had tears in my eyes. This was huge. Lee had no idea why I was so speechless.

When Ellen, his Sooner Start therapist, came back for the next weekly therapy visit, she saw a big change in Christopher. She was dumbfounded. "This type of change does not happen like this. It can take years of therapies; if it ever changes."

"I think it is a miracle," I said.

Roger used to caution me about saying things that make me sound like some religious nut, but I knew it was a miracle. I had the 'before and after' Christopher on video. Ellen could not explain it either, and agreed it must be a miracle. Roger and I thought back over the past couple of weeks to try to remember what happened.

Then we both said, "Sister Aemiliane!" Sister Aemiliane was a nun that had visited our church on a couple of occasions. She herself was a miracle, having been spared from death in 1981 after the skywalk of the Kansas City Hyatt Regency collapsed on top of her and crushed her spine. She had come to tell her story a few years prior and had been such a holy and comforting presence.

The only skin showing from her head to toe black habit and veil was her beautiful, glorious, luminous face. She said few words, but her eyes spoke volumes. Anastasia knew of Christopher's issues, although most just thought Christopher was shy or sleepy when he buried his head into the crook of our necks when they approached.

She said, "Let's have Sister Aemiliane pray over Christopher."

Fine, I thought. I was always open to anyone's extra prayers. Because we were not raised in evangelical churches, we were not big believers in 'laying on of hands' or anything you may see on television regarding an altar call for people with ailments to come forward to be prayed over. For me, being prayed over was just another person asking for God to bless another.

I was not expecting anything. It was just a nun in the middle of a chaotic coffee and donut hour coming by to say a little prayer over our son. Anastasia led her to our table and I told her a little about what was going on with the kids. She had remembered our plight from the last time she was in town. She didn't know anything about Christopher's anxiety.

The priest's wife, Presbytera Vicky, Marla and Anastasia were the only people around besides Roger and me. I was holding Christopher in my arms, and as usual, he was clinging on to me like a fearful cat. I could not see his face, but Roger could.

Sister Aemiliane said nothing. The room went quiet around me, but no one else noticed anything going on. She stroked his little soft chubby cheeks and I felt the cat-like grip start to loosen on me as Christopher relaxed more and more.

She continued to pray quietly as Roger watched

Christopher's face go from wincing and pain to soft and peaceful. I could tell something was happening, as the looks on Marla and Presbytera Vicky's faces were intent and their eyes glistened. What was happening that I couldn't see? It was all so fast.

Sister Aemiliane looked into my eyes as Christopher was totally relaxed and said, "He's going to be all right."

Roger saw Christopher take a deep breath and let it out, and that was the first time he had seen him relax. Just like that. I was grateful for the prayer, but I really didn't know what it meant. Until I watched Christopher jump off of that fireplace hearth into the arms of the handyman.

He is going to be all right.

39

STARBUCKS PAYS OFF

It turns out, my new vice wasn't all bad. You never know who you will see as you wait for your drink at Starbucks. When I could find a parking spot, I'd stop at the Starbucks near our house. Having grown up in Oklahoma City, I usually saw someone I knew. One day, I saw Jim Milner, standing in line, waiting for his coffee.

Jim was our lobbyist when I was president of the city chapter of my professional organization. I didn't know him well, other than a few brief meetings. We made small talk as we waited in line, and he asked what was going on. Over the course of the adoption, I had told everyone I knew the condensed version of the adoption failure, and the incredulous child support issue. Jim was more than interested.

He jumped right in and offered, "I know someone that might be able to help you. Senator Ron Peters deals with Department of Human Services (DHS) appropriations and he might like to help with legislation about the support issue. I'll get a meeting set up for you."

Another God wink. God knew I really needed my coffee that morning. Roger and I couldn't believe it. Legislation? I had practically grown up at the State Capitol. My mother was a secretary for a State Representative, and I had worked as a Page taking notes, coffee and water to various Representatives on the House floor.

It felt like home when I walked in the beautiful, historic building. I remembered the smell, the cold, hard marble that echoed when your high heels made contact and you clickety-clacked down the long halls.

In my former job, I frequently attended capitol committee meetings with our company and lobbyists. I had also lobbied for health care issues when I attended my professional organizations lobbying events at the Capitol.

State government is an amazing process. The lobbyists talk so fast, go from cell phone call, to call waiting, to meeting, to talking with each other about what is about to happen to bills on the floor, all with lightening speed. I absorbed it like a sponge, even though it made my head spin.

Senator Peters was delightful. He was so interested in our plight and said he had a current bill that we could add wording to. As his bill could not help us with our current case, he wanted to make sure the definition of child support in an adoption situation was tightened up to ensure that what happened to us, didn't happen to anyone else. He asked us to have Noel write our wording for the proposed amendment to the current law. We got it to him a few days later, and were on our way. We also needed a Senate co-sponsor, just in case our house bill did not make it. We knew exactly who to call!

40

THE SENATOR

It always helps to have connections. *Even if you have forgotten you have them.* You never know when those connections will come in handy. Being the industrious guy that he is, Roger decided as a teen to work for his teacher and football coach. Coach Crutchfield ran a lawn business during the summer months, and became a father figure to Roger, as Roger's father had died when he was twelve.

Who could have imagined that this small town teacher and lawn services owner, Coach Crutchfield, would go on to become one of the most powerful Senators in the State of Oklahoma.

Senator Crutchfield is larger than life in stature and spirit. He also was adopted, and didn't find out until he was over fifty years old. Ironically, he was also of Indian heritage. He commented that he wouldn't be where he was today if things hadn't happened exactly the way they did in his life, and he had no regrets about having been placed for adoption.

When Roger called his old mentor to tell him about our adoption plight, what we had been through up to this point and the law we wanted to amend, we discovered Senator Crutchfield had gone to college with Chief Pyle. Another coincidence or God wink? Or, in Senator Crutchfield's words, "It is an injustice to humanity to call things coincidences."

Senator Crutchfield's help was like one of his hugs; a feeling everything was going to be all right. We had a sense of stepping back and seeing our life as a beautiful tapestry with both of our stories and lives interwoven.

Senator Crutchfield also knew another Senator with a spot in one of her bills for our language. Senator Mary Easley, a kind-hearted lady, had served in the Senate for many years. We liked her instantly and knew that she was going to help us all she could.

Having never followed bills from creation to being signed into law, this was a huge learning process. I loved every minute of it. It was another positive distraction from the worrying about what could happen to Christopher and Abby if we did not prevail. After we had bill numbers and a date, we then had to wait until the date the bill would come up for a vote. Now it was time to lobby.

This was not Roger's bag, but it was mine. He went with me a few times, but felt there was so much ground to cover, it was like being a door-to-door salesman. He supported me from afar and waited to hear what went on every night after we put the kids to bed.

My high school friend, Erin, now a professional photographer in Tennessee, had put together the most beautiful Christmas card for us. The kids had these angelic sweet expressions on their faces as Christopher rested his head on the shoulder of Abby's red velvet dress. I took this card with me as I made the rounds to put a picture with names of the children that were being impacted by a law that needed clarification.

How could they not vote for this bill? There was really nothing to argue. The bill clarified that in an adoption situation, when parental rights are being terminated, child support paid by the biological parent must benefit the child, and could not be used for drug testing, DNA testing, counseling or anything else that benefitted only the biological parent.

I estimated that ninety-nine percent of the Senators and Representatives that I spoke with, (and I did speak with almost all of them), were incredulous that a judge would rule the way our judge had.

This is when I learned the phrase 'legislated from the bench,' meaning the judge decided how to interpret a law the way he wanted to rule. No one had previously interpreted the law this way, and legislators I spoke with were surprised at the ruling.

The law went through the gyrations, with us there every step of the way, proud to be a part of the process. When I asked to speak to the Representative or Senator, the assistants would always ask which group I was with. Most were surprised when I told them I was there on my children's behalf as a private citizen. I guess they don't get that very often.

Having done it, I am amazed there aren't more private citizens doing the same thing for their own causes. People are willing to listen if you are passionate about something that makes sense.

2007

FINDING OUR WAY

41

UPDATES AND BIRTH MOTHER HUGS

Email Update - 01/24/07

Dear Friends and Family
The court hearing set for Friday was a result of us losing our last hearing. The normal process for a failed adoption, which is what we have now, is to set a Custody Hearing. We will go in front of the judge to request a 'Stay,' which means we want to put off the Custody Hearing, pending the outcome of our Appeal.

We filed a 'Petition in Error,' basically telling the Appellate Court that we think the District Judge was wrong in ruling that the birth father's paying for drug testing and court-ordered payment of supervised visitation due to his being on Meth, is considered child support, and thus gives the birth father the right to stop the adoption.

If the District Court refuses our request for the Stay, we have the right to go to the State Supreme Court to request a Stay. I hope that one way or another, we will get things put off until our Appeal can run its course.

We will also be asking the judge to set arrearages (the dollar amount the birth father owes in back child support, insurance, day care, etc...) which currently is a small fortune.

We are also working on legislation to help tighten up the wording on what is considered child support--and how child support must directly benefit the children. We will let you know when we have a bill number to follow.

Christopher is now ranging out, getting up in the middle of the night to explore the refrigerator and the flour sifter (his new favorite), as well as copying Curious George antics like completely unrolling the toilet paper.

Abby has a new room and a new big girl bed, but refuses to sleep in it. She sleeps on the floor, half under the bed with various fire trucks and toys under her covers. After Christopher is asleep, she sneaks into his room, takes his nightlight and puts it in her bed. She is tricky!

Love,
Valerie, Roger, Abby and Christopher

Email Update - 01/26/07

Dear Friends and Family,
I am happy to report that we don't have court tomorrow!! As much as it stresses us out when the birth father throws a wrench in the process, delays are in our favor, as we can have Abby and Christopher longer, and there is less disruption of their lives. Luckily, we haven't caused a delay yet, so they cannot say we have been dragging this out. Prayers are answered in unexpected ways.

Love,
Valerie, Roger, Abby and Christopher

P.S. I have been a little preoccupied---I must have missed the 'note in the tote' that today was class picture day at the kids' school. *Mine were dressed in their 'best' sweatpants and t-shirts ready to get dirty, and Abby was sporting her first shiner from a run in with the fireplace hearth. Being the perfectionist that I am, it was pretty funny to see all of the other kids in their perfect matching outfits and hair bows, ready for the camera. Things really are in perspective about what is important in life!!*

Email to Nicole - 02/22/07

Hi Nicole,
We had a very exciting day today at the Capitol. Our House Bill 1576 and our Senate Bill 469 both passed the floor today. We were there watching and it brought tears to my eyes. We are halfway towards having a law to define child support as actually benefiting the child!! The kids will be so excited to open more presents. They love that. We will keep you in our prayers, as always.

Love,
Valerie, Roger, Abby and Christopher

Email from Nicole – 02/23/2007

Hi Valerie,
Thanks for updating me on the Bills you are trying to get passed. That is really exciting about your House Bill 1576 and Senate Bill 469 passing the floor! I was wondering how that was going. I hope that everything works out for the best. That would be really great! I will be praying for you!

Love,
Nicole

Email from Nicole - 03/14/07

Dear Valerie and Roger,
Thank you so much for the pictures of Abby and Christopher!
It amazes me how much they have changed over the years! They are really developing into beautiful young children! Also, I wanted to tell you how much I appreciate the cards from Abby and Christopher! Each one touched my heart in a special way and made me cry. It means so much to me to get pictures and letters from you. I am really grateful to you both for doing it.

I can see that Abby and Christopher are loved and cared for very much! I thank God everyday for putting you and Roger in my life at the time I needed you the most. I feel that it was God's Will for you and Roger to be blessed as the parents for Abby and Christopher.

I am so grateful that the twins are with two wonderful, loving parents who can provide them with the best life possible! You and Roger are my angels!

Thank you very much from the bottom of my heart.

Love,
Nicole

42

GREEN Y'S

Email Update - 03/16/07

Dear Friends and Family,
As we watched the 'scoreboard' light up with all green 'Y's and not one red 'N' during the vote on the floor of the House of Representatives, we know we are one step closer to having a new law defining what child support is and is not. We had no idea how thrilling it would be to watch this happen in person.

We now start working on the Senate side to make sure it passes through committee before going to the Senate floor for a full vote. Thank you so much for making those contacts with your legislators!

Love,

Valerie, Roger, Abby and Christopher

Email Update – 04/06/2007

Dear Family, Friends and Co-Workers,
Well, we had one of our bills, House
Bill (HB) 1576, killed before it got to the
Senate committee. It died at the hands
of a Senator who was using the bill as a
political maneuver. We don't have all the
details, but apparently it did not have
enough weight to be heard at the same
time as the Immigration bill.

However, all is not lost, as SB 469
(Sen. Easley's bill) passed unanimously
in the Senate, and will be heard by the
Human Services Committee in the next
week or so. If you recall, HB 1576 was
sponsored by a member of the Judiciary
Committee, and he tells us we have a
good shot. If you know a Representative
on the Committee, please call them within
the next week to ask for their support of
SB 469.

We go to court next Tuesday,
April 10. Items on the docket include a
Petition for Stay, which will put off any
Custody Hearing pending the outcome
of our Appeal decision. (The Appeal

was filed and we are waiting on it to be assigned to an Appellate Division.) We will also discuss child support arrearages. It is a substantial amount, which the birth father must pay, regardless of the outcome of the Appeal.

As for an update on the kids, Abby is still mad at me for taking her choo choo train birthday cake leftovers to work, and reminds me every time Christopher brings it up, or she sees it on the computer slide show. Her face wrinkles up in disgust as she declares "Mommy took MY cake to work."

Christopher loves to count. I can't tell him I will count to three before he goes for a time out, because he continues to count with abandon and excitement past three up to almost twenty! He wants to read the newspaper so he can point out the numbers in the sale ads. He sees numbers in everything we do, including the keyhole in the breakfast chair shaped like a figure 8. I'm sure it won't be long before Roger has him learning to play poker.

Love,
Valerie, Roger, Abby and Christopher

Email Update – 04/10/07

Hello Friends and Family,
It has been a busy and exhausting day. For those of you who don't know, our House Bill 1576 never made it to the Senate committee after being passed unanimously out of the House. We understand that the co-chair of the committee had a problem with judges not being able to have more leeway and he didn't want it heard. He is a former tribal judge himself.

It was very surprising, since it took nothing away from a biological parent, and it just held them more accountable to do something to benefit a child. The good news is that our Senate Bill 469 passed unanimously out of the Senate and onto the House. Today, we went to the House meeting to see it pass through committee. No opposition! It will now go to the House floor for a full vote in the next week. So, CALL YOUR HOUSE REPRESENTATIVE (not Senator) and tell them that you urge their support of SB 469--it passed unanimously out of the Senate and unanimously out of the Human Services Committee.

Also, remind them it is the same amendatory language they voted unanimously for in HB 1576 a few weeks ago. We are so grateful to Rep. Ron Peters who authored the first HB 1576, and co-authored SB 469, and is the Chair of the Human Services Committee.

If it passes the floor of the House, it will go back to the Senate since the title was stricken, and then put back on in committee. We understand there will be no room for debating the issue on the Senate floor once it gets there.

Whew! We are getting a real life lesson in how our system works. You have to be on top of it daily and in the faces of the representatives, constantly educating them on the issues. (Let me know if you need another email with bullet talking points that I sent out previously).

Court update....well, it was strange. We did not have a hearing. The judge decided that procedurally there needs to be a Custody Hearing since the adoption failed. We disagreed because we have an Appeal pending, and the outcome could change everything. He is waiting on briefs arguing both sides from both parties. We will have another hearing on June 15, regardless of the outcome of the briefs.

We are confident that our argument will win, but it will be taxing nonetheless. It seems absurd to do this, since the outcome of the Appeal will be out within a month of this hearing, and may change the outcome of the judge's decision! But we still have mountains of faith, two precious reminders of why we are fighting so hard, and all of you holding us up daily. Thank you, thank you!!!

Love,
Valerie, Roger, Abby and Christopher

Email to Nicole - 04/10/07

Hi Nicole,
We have a committee meeting in the morning to get one of our bills passed and I will fill you in at court. I am looking forward to seeing you tomorrow and seeing how things are going for you. You, as always, are my hero and such a trooper. I still feel positive about things and the faith God has given me to endure the long stretch. I pray you do too!

Love,
Valerie, Roger, Abby and Christopher

Email From Nicole- 04/10/07

Dear Valerie and Roger,
Thanks so much for the message and the pictures of Abby and Christopher! The pics turned out just fine! It was good to see you and Roger at court today. It has been about eight months since the last court date. I feel that today went well in court, and that we have many options. We just have to sit back and wait to see what the judge is going to do.

Nicole

Email Update - 05/03/07

Dear Friends and Family,
Just a quick update of some very important things going on....
#1. See the featured article in this coming Sunday's Business Section of The Oklahoman. We have been interviewed about the cost of adoption. Our angle is about the unexpected costs of legal fees in addition to the adoption fees. It will be good to get some positive press at this point of the game.
#2. We are holding our breath for the next couple of days. Our Senate Bill 469

has gone through its many gyrations successfully, and is sitting on the Governor's desk for signature, which he must do by Friday. When this happens, we will have CHANGED A LAW that defines what is and is not child support as it relates to parents whose parental rights are being terminated in an adoption situation. #3. Finally, and most important: Abby and Christopher are nearly potty-trained!

Love,
Valerie, Roger, Abby and Christopher

Journal - 05/29/09

Abby and Christopher played in the dirt helping Roger garden. Christopher wanted to run into the street and Abby wanted to get her hands and feet covered with dirt while searching for sticks and old mulch under the dirt. They are so opposite! Christopher doesn't want to get any dirt on him!

We took them to the mall. They love the blue jewel-adorned buffalo outside of BC Clark's jewelry store. They love to pat its nose and side.

ADOPTION: THE UNPAVED ROAD TO HAPPINESS   **189**

43

OUR NEW LAW

Senate Bill 469 was signed into law. We took Christopher and Abby to the Capitol to have their picture made with Senators Easley and Crutchfield, and Representative Ron Peters. They took us back to a room behind the Senate Chambers and had animal crackers for Christopher and Abby. The Senate photographer took several photos of us, which everyone later signed and sent to us. They hang proudly in our home.

The highway to downtown passes right by the Capitol and every time we drive by, Abby points and yells, "Look mommy, we've been there. We changed the law." I still get a lump in my throat when she does that since the first time she said it she was not even four years old. Maybe politics will be in her blood.

Unfortunately, as good as it feels to change the law for others that may be in the same circumstances, it does nothing to help our current situation. The law is not retroactive. However, if we happen to lose the Appeal, it may help us in the long run.

Email Update - 05/30/09

Dear Friends and Family,

Governor Henry signed State Bill 469 into law a couple of weeks ago. It will take effect in November of this year. This is a major victory of which we are very proud and excited. You have all been such a big part of this cheering us on, making phone calls on Christopher and Abby's behalf and keeping the prayers going.

There was overwhelming support, with 99.9% passage by both the House and the Senate. If you are so inclined, you may call, write or email Representative Ron Peters and Senator Mary Easley, both of Tulsa, to thank them (and your respective legislator and the Governor as well).

Currently, we are waiting on our judge to decide if we have to have a Custody Hearing in the interim before the decision is reached by the Court of Civil Appeals.

At this point, we are praying we don't have to go in that direction.

Meanwhile, Abby and Christopher

are in training for the Ultimate Fighting Championship wrestling match. Abby seems to be taking the lead with more moves, but Christopher is learning how to run quickly before she gets him pinned down.

Love,
Valerie, Roger, Abby and Christopher

44

APPEAL VICTORY

Email Update - 06/06/07

Dear Friends and Family,
WE WON THE APPEAL! What does that
mean? It means that two out of three
Court of Appeals judges sided with us
and against the District Court's previous
decision. His ruling was REVERSED
AND REMANDED.
  *That being said, it is **not** over.*
  There are a few factors involved, one
being the ICWA. As you may recall, this
is a federal law that tries to protect kids
with Indian blood from being taken from
biological parents. This law stipulates a
Placement Preference; beginning with
blood relatives and down about seventh

on the list would be 'other tribe members and foster parents.'

From early on, the Choctaw Nation indicated that they would not request a Placement Preference, then later changed their minds and said that the kids were 'fine where they are' for now, and they would let the District (non-Indian) Court decide what to do.

If they decide to change their minds on Placement Preference, will we be in more of a custody battle with the birth father's family.

The other factor is the hearing set for June 15 to determine how much back child support, the birth father legally owes. It is up to almost $40,000, but the judge can knock that down. Even if it is cut in half, that debt does not go away due to bankruptcy or any other factor, and the birth father's wages will be garnished from any job he has in the future.

Or, it might go away if the birth father decides not to pursue any further recourse of the ICWA. Your prayers are working, and we feel that the end is really in sight. I do hope you pray for both the birth mother (Dean's Honor Roll!!) AND the birth father, as they have both produced such a gift of beautiful, precious children that would not be where they are without them.

In different ways, they have sacrificed a lot. We are so grateful for all of the challenges and trials, as it makes us so appreciative of what we have. We would do it all over again and again. Thank you all for sharing your concern and being there for the defeats and FINALLY an important victory!!

Love,
Valerie, Roger, Abby and Christopher

P.S. The kids and I were talking about who is a girl and who is a boy. I said, "Abby is a girl and Christopher is a boy. Mommy is a girl and Daddy is a boy. Actually Mommy is a lady and Daddy is a man." Abby didn't miss a beat and said, "Mommy, you're no lady, and Daddy is an old man." Ouch.

Christopher is still on the losing end of the Ultimate Fighting Championship, as Abby literally boxed his sore infected ears and poked him in the eye while he was sleeping, leaving a red, sore eye. Poor guy! He will be after her soon!

Email from Nicole - 06/07/07

Hello Valerie,

I heard the good news about winning the Appeal!!! It is exciting! I wanted to jump up and down and scream when my parents told me! It was a big relief to hear that news although I know this isn't over with just yet! However, I can see the light at the end of the tunnel and things are looking promising!!!

I have faith that God will lead us all through according to His Will! I truly believe that He wants Abby and Christopher to be adopted by you and Roger and sees that you both are the best parents for them. I feel that God blessed me by placing you and Roger in my life when I needed it the most! You both are my angels!!

Abby and Christopher are so blessed and fortunate to have wonderful, loving parents like you and Roger! That is so amazing that the decision was made on your mother's 81st birthday! I bet June 1st will be a very special day and will be treasured by you!

Thank you all so much for keeping my parents as well as myself updated with all that is going on with the case!

We really appreciate it! The pictures are great too!

Nicole

45

WAITING ON THE SUPREME COURT

Email Update - 09/28/07

Dear Friends and Family,
Who would have thought it would get this far? I have joked that the kids would be in kindergarten before this was over, and I may be right! Since it has been a very long while since I have sent out an email, I will bring you quickly up to speed.

* *The District Court ruled in favor of the birth father, saying that his paying for court ordered drug tests and supervised visitation constituted child support and we could not adopt the kids without his consent.*

* *We appealed and WON. The Court of Appeals agreed that anything that the birth father did for himself did not benefit the kids and they ruled that we didn't need his permission/consent to adopt the kids.*

* *The birth father has appealed the Court of Appeals decision to the State Supreme Court of Oklahoma. We understand that less than five percent of the cases brought to the State Supreme Court even get reviewed. Most are left untouched, as the parameters for the State Supreme Court to take on a case for review are pretty major. For example, there must be arguments made in the request for review that establish that the Court of Appeals erred in their decision, that the case is a landmark type case that has never been visited and would set strong precedent for future cases, etc. According to our attorney, the brief written by the birth father's attorney didn't meet these criteria.*

* *The State Supreme Court decides to grant Certiorari (a legal appeal of a judicial decision) and review the case.*

They have six months to review and render an opinion.

* *In the meantime, we went to the State Capitol, lobbied and changed a law to say child support in an adoption situation must benefit the child. This will go into effect November 1, 2007, but cannot be used in our case retroactively. So, we are again in a holding pattern to see what the State Supreme Court does. They have many options. They may just write an opinion on the case. There are nine State Supreme Court justices and five must rule the same way. Even if they do not rule favorably, we still have other avenues in place to accomplish our ultimate goal, and then we may also be able to use the new law we helped pass for our own benefit.*

We are a little grayer, a little wiser, and if you can get even more determined, we are that too. Good will prevail. I hope the unpaved road on which we travel will clearly show our trail for the next naïve souls that follow.

The kids are hilarious and keep us so on track. They now pray every night.

*"We love you Jesus; Thy will be done."
We ask for your prayers to be the same.
Christopher can't quite say Thy will, so
he says, 'We love you Jesus, and I will be
done.' Yes, Christopher, that about sums
it up.*

*And we close with the most
important reason for the email...
the kids. Christopher's new fashion
statement is a row of about ten 'Cars'
or 'Finding Nemo' Band-Aids lining the
front of his legs. I don't like the person
who invented those! What happened
to the flesh colored ones?? These are
waterproof and you can't get near him
to take them off! If they do come off,
you are just left with rings of sticky dirt.
Abby is boy crazy and each day she
comes home talking about her newest
love, usually the one with the most
recent birthday party and the best
cake. We are already worried about
her. She will have dated her whole
school before first grade, and the
school goes up to the twelfth grade!!*

*Thank you for all of your prayers,
support, emails, and uplifting thoughts.
We are the luckiest people in the
world and are blessed beyond belief!*

Love,
Valerie, Roger, Abby and Christopher

Email from Susan - 08/16/07

Valerie,
When I read your email, my first thought was "Why?" Then I remembered my favorite Zen proverb..."when we understand, things are just as they are and when we don't understand, things are just as they are." I guess we aren't going to know why...but like you, I continue to trust in our Lord...and pray for His mother's intercession. I pray that she will help you and Roger stay strong during these times that continue to be so trying. Know that each day on the way to work, I pray for your family. Take heart and know that you are all loved!

Peace,
Susan

2008

THE END OF THE ROAD

46

AND THE WINNER IS...

We were told the State Supreme Court could take up to six months to make a decision on the Appeal that we won. Will the justices affirm or reverse the lower court decision? After almost four years, it is a waiting game. We look at the bright side of delays; more time makes it that much harder to argue that it is in Christopher and Abby's best interest to be taken from our care and placed anywhere else.

Because we were prepared for the six-month mark, we were not expecting the call from Noel after just three months telling us that the State Supreme Court had decided not to look at the case, as had been requested by the birth father after losing his appeal. When she first told us, I didn't quite grasp the meaning immediately, as her tone was rather nonchalant. I was in a pattern of automatic disbelief when something sounded too good to be true.

"Repeat that, please?" I said.

"The decision of the Court of Appeals stands. You can adopt Christopher and Abby without the consent of the birth father. We can terminate his rights," said Noel.

"Is it really over?" I asked. I guess I expected confetti to drop out of the ceiling, or to hear angels sing, or at least to break through that runners tape at the end of this marathon. It was over. I think I was in shock.

Email Update - 03/05/08

Dear Friends and Family,

I have been hesitant to give an update lately, as there were so many things happening and so many balls in the air. But believe it or not, after four years of changing diapers and changing laws, it looks like things may be coming to an end! We are scheduled to appear before the judge at 11:00 a.m. on Monday, March 10th for him to sign off on the Best Interest of the Child order. I say sign off instead of our having a full-blown hearing. (In December, the State Supreme Court decided that they did not want to review the birth father's Appeal.) This decision means we CAN terminate the parental rights of the birth father, and we can adopt Abby and Christopher without his permission.

The birth mother has put herself through college, earned a degree (with honors) in Psychology, and is now counseling troubled youth. She has been a hero to us with her unwavering support.

I will keep you posted after Monday's events, but please pray that no last minute snags pop up! If everything goes smoothly, we can FINALIZE the adoption forever – the day before the kids turn four!

Love,

Valerie, Roger, Abby and Christopher

47

IT'S OFFICIAL

Until now, Christopher and Abby had been spared the many visits to the courthouse. But today was different. The judge wanted them there, in person. It wasn't that they needed to sign anything, but it was a happy day, the day the judge made our family official.

Christopher had been doing great since our little miracle a few years back, but he must have Roger-dar, and sensed that something was not right. He had a bad feeling about that courthouse. We came within a few feet of the building, and he threw a fit. He resisted and cried. We cajoled and carried him. He was suspicious of the metal detector he had to go through. He hated the waiting room. He didn't want to go in the courtroom, so the judge let us go into his small chambers.

Abby was on Roger's lap, Christopher was on mine. He squirmed and fidgeted, would not pay attention and tried to get away from me while the judge read his official legalese. It was not until the judge called us 'forever family' that Christopher calmed down and looked peacefully at the judge and smiled.

Journal - 03/17/08

What can I say? After tomorrow it is OVER! Last Monday the judge ruled that we are FOREVER FAMILY. Christopher and Abby turned four on Tuesday, we celebrated with our church family on the Sunday of Orthodoxy and tomorrow we have closure with Catholic Charities and our hero, Nicole.

As much as Nicole has wanted to see the twins, out of respect for our feelings, she had not asked to see them until everything was final and they were permanently and forever in our care.
I sent her a card saying:

> *I knew in my heart this day would come and this journey would end, yet I had no idea it would take so long. I would do it all over again for so many reasons. We are so proud of you. We knew you were special from the day we met you, and knew you had to be such a strong person to choose life over convenience. What you have*

done is the most self-sacrificing, inconvenient gift a person can give, and we are so eternally grateful for your choosing to let God guide and direct us to be the best family for Christopher and Abby.

You can be assured that they will be given a life of opportunity, with strong boundaries, love, faith and lessons in humility, compassion and principles, and of course, just having fun being kids. We will explore the world together, making them feel special and part of a much large part of God's plan. We don't know how else to express our gratitude to you, except to strive to raise these precious children in Christ's likeness according to His will for them.

They will know Him, and they will know His blessed Mother Mary, as they will know her ultimate sacrifice for the love of her Son. They will know the depth of your ultimate sacrifice for them. Giving them life, and through us, the best life possible.

On our way home from court, Christopher said with a smile, "Mommy, Daddy, Abby, Christopher and

Pwimwose, (the dog), we're a fangley."
Yes, Christopher, we are a forever
fangley after all!

48

THE FINAL VISIT

Catholic Charities had been our matchmaker, our match made in heaven, our date from Hell, and finally, our mother-of-the-bride. They were hosting an adoption party for us, since most of the agency knew us by now, mostly as, *those poor people*! They all knew the story of Christopher and Abby and were so happy to have it over with.

I was a little apprehensive to bring Christopher and Abby to the place where they had visitation and were so anxious, so many times. But that was long ago, and I hoped their little memories would not hold those images. They were having balloons and cake, which I knew they both loved so much. And Nicole was going to be there.

This was going to be so hard for her. I was so very proud of her enduring this for so long, as she tried to put herself through college studying psychology. She wanted to help others, especially troubled youth. I wanted her to see how loved and cared for Christopher and Abby were, and give her that closure that she had needed for so long.

She sat down to eat cake. Christopher was preoccupied with his icing and the balloons. Abby sat across the table from her, looking intently into Nicole's face. Could she see herself? She just smiled and jabbered.

Nicole couldn't do it at first. She had to leave the room to compose herself, seeing herself in them, their faces, and their little souls. I thought that was all she was going to be able to handle, but she said she wanted to go upstairs to the playroom, away from all of the people, and watch them play.

Abby and Christopher went straight for the playhouse, climbing in and out, and making food on the play stove. Nicole observed from afar, slowly inching closer. She finally sat down on the floor while they played, gently interacting with them. She started to smile, then laugh and have fun. I believe she was finally at peace knowing Abby and Christopher were where they were meant to be.

EPILOGUE

God's Will

The adoption ordeal marked the first time in my life that I had ever prayed for God's will instead of my own. I figured it was time to try a new way of praying as my old way just wasn't working. Just praying "Thy will be done" was simple and I figured it would lessen my chances for disappointment when expectations I set were not met. My prayers over the years were like asking Santa to decide what I should have for Christmas instead of me sending an itemized list of everything I wanted.

When we initially prayed, I said "God, if this is your will for us (to adopt), make it easy." Well, this was one of those combo prayers where I asked for his will, but I put in some parameters. He did hear our prayer and did make it easy in the beginning. But my prayer had also covered the other side of the fence, "If it is not your will and not meant to be, make it hard". He did that too, as you have read. Very hard.

Roger didn't know what I was praying, nor did I know his prayers, until later in the game when I admitted to the line of conditions that I had set out before God. I was to learn a lot about the man I married throughout our adoption. I knew he was a private man, and knew too that he was not outwardly spiritual. He didn't like spontaneous praying out loud or raising hands in prayer at church. I didn't know the depth of his spirituality until we fought our fight together. He had a different theory, and I now know it was the best approach.

Roger reminded me that everything worth having does not come easy. He said that while we really weren't sure what we wanted, God had placed Abby and Christopher in our lives with us knowing we would have to fight, proving to ourselves and to God that it was what we really wanted. God gives us the opportunity, we make it happen. "If it is too easy, we will not appreciate it," Roger said, "and if you are not willing to work for something, you must not want it very badly."

I then read Romans 8:16-17.

The Spirit himself testifies with our spirit that we are God's children. Now if we are children, then we are heirs, heirs of God and co-heirs with Christ, if indeed we share in his sufferings in order that we may also share in his glory.

And, Romans 8:26-27.

In the same way, the spirit helps us in our weakness. We do not know what we ought to pray for, but the Spirit himself intercedes for us with groans that words cannot express. And he who searches our hearts knows the mind of the Spirit because the Spirit intercedes for the saints in accordance with God's will.

There it was again. God's will. All of those beautiful words can be boiled down to two...simple....words. Talk about cutting to the chase!

Now looking back on our journey without the intense emotional impact, we understand how the

Choctaw's first response was to support a biological parent in accordance with the ICWA. The tribe has a legal and historic interest to protect their members and their offspring, to preserve their culture and heritage, and provide ethical and legal protection.

I feel certain that it was difficult for the Chief of the tribe, after being inundated by us and others, to make the decision he did to withdraw support of one member and become neutral on the issue. He had to weigh and balance what was best for the twins as well as his responsibility to preserve the historic culture of an Indian Nation. The tribe and Native American culture has made great contributions to our society, communities and their members. And, it remains their goal to have children with Indian blood appreciate and understand the difficult path that was built before them.

From the beginning, almost everyone told us that our adoption case was unusual, and that it would not turn out in our favor. However, Roger and I steadfastly believed in miracles aided by God's hand, and also in God's guidance, grace and direction to fight for these precious children. Every case is different and our encouragement for those who come after us is never to give up hope, to pray for God's direction and will, and to reach out to friends and family for resources and prayers.

To Christopher and Abby:

Eleven

Eleven is my lucky number
It is the day I met you, in the third month.
They are the numbers 1 and 1 that form the "11"
between my eyebrows,
the wrinkles I earned from years of thoughts about you.
They are a perfect match; mirror images, identical, yet
indivisible;
Individual, yet a pair to go hand in hand, side by side,
Perfect, symmetrical, odd;
Standing at attention
Waiting to be noon, or a dozen, or an even number.
But in my mind,
Only to rhyme with heaven,
Which is where I have been,
Since the day you were born
and the day you became officially
Forever family.

Oklahoma Senate Bill 469

B. Consent to adoption is not required from a parent who, for a period of twelve (12) consecutive months out of the last fourteen (14) months immediately preceding the filing of a petition for adoption of a child or a petition to terminate parental rights pursuant to Section 7505-2.1 of this title, has willfully failed, refused, or neglected to contribute to the support of such minor:

1. In substantial compliance with an order entered by a court of competent jurisdiction adjudicating the duty, amount, and manner of support; or

2. According to such parent's financial ability to contribute to such minor's support if no provision for support is provided in an order. For the purposes of this section, support for the minor shall benefit the minor by providing a necessity. Payments that shall not be considered support shall include, but are not limited to:

     a. genetic and drug testing,

     b. supervised visitation,

     c. counseling for any person other than the minor,

     d. court fees and costs,

     e. restitution payments, and

     f. transportation costs for any person other than the minor, unless such transportation expenses are specifically ordered in lieu of support in a court order.

Acknowledgements

To the Lord above.
Thank you for directing us to this unpaved road and gently guiding us along the way. Friends, family and complete strangers along our path were like bread crumbs to follow when we were wandering aimlessly, as were your random God winks to acknowledge that we were going in the right direction. How freeing it is to just pray for Thy Will Be Done!

To my amazing husband.
Roger, words cannot even begin to express my gratitude and love for you. There is no one else I would rather have at my side, and watching my back.

To my family.
My love to my wonderful mother, Mercedes (Muzzie) for adopting me and setting the example of courageously getting involved, and changing things for the better. And to her husband, 'Papa' Leroy for the love and constant support of our family, and for standing silently and solidly by our sides. To my deceased father Papa Lew. For adopting me, encouraging me and loving me and my family. To my siblings Fred and Teresa and their families, Roger's siblings Cynthia, Harry, Robert and Tom, their spouses and children, for being our prayer partners and cheerleaders.

To Nicole. Thank you from the bottom of my heart. This book is in your honor, and is truly a love story. And, to your parents, who hung with us, in good times and bad.

To Sabra, our guardian angel social worker, who guided us through the unfamiliar and turbulent waters of adoption while providing comfort and encouragement, and the connection to Nicole.

To Noel Tucker and her husband Phil for battling it out for us in the courtroom; always finding new angles to approach our delicate issues. To Nicole's attorney, Jack, who was in our corner helping us all the way.

To Ray and Walter Merchant for their loving fostering in the first few weeks of the babies' lives.

To Father John for his prayers, encouragement and communication to our church family.

To Sister Aemiliane (now Abbess Aemiliane) for her prayers and intercessions and her calming presence in our tulmultous life.

To Rolanda Walker Smith (RoRo), our steadfast nanny that helped us make it through the day. We couldn't have done it without you.

To Senator Johnny Crutchfield for providing Roger with an outstanding example and role model in his early years. We are grateful for your leadership and encouragement, your perspective as an adoptee, and as a Native American. Thank you for helping us change the law.

To Representative Ron Peters for taking on our issue and seeing it through to fruition. Thank you for taking on tough children's issues! To Senator Mary Easley, for taking the issue on in SB469. You made it possible for us to make a difference.

To Linda Lambert for inadvertently pairing me with seasoned and spirited women (especially Jeanne Hoffman Smith) who gave me the kick in the pants I needed to actually put my story on paper.

To Katie Gordy, Retreat Facilitator and spiritual advisor, friend and inspiration, who provided me with two creative and productive silent retreats in which to write in peace and without interruption in the sacred space of Mount Saint Mary's.

To Lolly Anderson, my friend, mentor and now publisher. Without your encouragement and guidance, I wouldn't have come this far!

To Cathy Miller, my editor. Thank you for being so patient with my perfectionist tendencies and helping me see the big picture.

To my ad hoc editiorial commentators, Greg, Leisa, Christa and Lindsey: thanks for your constructive comments and insight!

To the hundreds of friends, friends of friends, and strangers, who prayed for us without knowing us, who showered us with baby gifts, sent encouraging emails, made phone calls and intervened for us when it was needed.

To anyone I have accidentally left out, please know that you have been a part of this journey and we will always be forever grateful that you were in our lives when we needed you the most.

Finally, to the angels that we will encounter in the future, helping us to forge ahead, clearing the path for others, While our adoption is complete, our mission to help children and their families is not.

All proceeds from the sale of this book will be donated to the protection of children in adoption, foster and ICWA situations.